in the BECOMING

carrying on after life derails

Jocelyn Faire

Copyright © 2020 by Jocelyn Faire
First Edition — November 2020

ISBN
978-1-988983-13-4 (Paperback)
978-1-988983-14-1 (eBook)

All rights reserved.

Short portions of the author's words may be quoted without permission, but should be credited.

No part of this publication may be reproduced in any form, or by any means, electronic or mechanical, including photocopying, recording, or any information browsing, storage, or retrieval system, without permission in writing from the publisher.

Bible references from The Message (NavPress) unless otherwise noted.

Cover Design by Ellen Hooge
Cover photo Jocelyn Faire

Produced by

Siretona Creative
Calgary, AB, Canada
www.siretona.com

Distributed to the trade by The Ingram Book Company

in the
BECOMING

in the
BECOMING

In the Becoming was the girl, and the girl was with God,
and God was with the girl in becoming.
Darkness was upon her face.
As Spirit moved upon the face of the girl
without breath and void
and the void overtook.
In becoming, the girl took over
and wrestled with God
as deep called to deep
and in that moment
she struggled with the call
that remained
to become for a time, for a season
because the time would soon come
for her to
Be-coming home to herself.

೫ ೩

The walls you're rebuilding are never out of my sight.
Isaiah 49:16

Dedication

In everyone's life, at some time, our inner fire goes out. It is then burst into flame by an encounter with another human being. We should all be thankful for those people who rekindle the inner spirit.

Albert Schweitzer

- Precious to me are the many women who have rekindled my inner spirit on the *becoming* journey. This book is dedicated to those women, some named here.

- My deepest gratitude to my daughter on the planet, Kristen Naomi – you inspire and encourage, you radiate light. I am delighted to be your mother. Your ongoing reminder that my story wasn't finished yet has kept me going.

- My mother, Margaret Krahn – from you I learned to detest gossip and to maintain a positive attitude in difficult times. You sewed more than clothes for your children, you sewed love, perseverance, and celebration into our lives.

- My dear surrogate daughter, Nicky Wales – I was privileged to be called Mum by you. I wanted to tell you that you were named in my book, sadly you left too soon. See you in heaven.

- Rita, Edith, Gloria, Vicki, Debbie, Dorothy – as soul sisters you have shared tears and laughter adding immense beauty in a most *becoming* way. A special thank you to Rita for excellent editing input.

- Maisha – my granddaughter whose very name means *life*. May you continue your journey to *becoming* a beautiful young woman.

- My new daughters-in-law Michelle, Charlene, Heather – thank you for acceptance and love.

- Ingun, Judy in Australia, Carol, sweet Catherine, Kari – other mother hearts bonded through loss and inspiring in their tenacity.

- Madeleine, Eva, Penny, Karen, Audrey – new friends in new places.

- Thank you, Ellen – for cover design and encouragement to continue this project.

- Thank you, Colleen – for publishing support in a lovely personal manner.

- Thank you to many other women of character who add beauty to life through conversations, writing, supportive prayers and hugs. Because of you, we all smile more and cry less.

- I do thank one very special man in my life, Harold, for infusing my life with love, adventure, and belonging. What a gift!

Preamble

> *My, isn't she BECOMING ...*
> *But becoming what?*
>
> And the day came when the risk to remain tight in a bud was more painful than the risk it took to blossom. Life is a process of becoming, a combination of states we have to go through.
>
> Anaïs Nin

Becoming is a spiritually reflective look at life, in the aftermath of severe loss. Adversity comes in all shapes and sizes. From the moment we are born we are trained to expect adversity, trained to overcome it. But there are times when it overcomes us. And where do we go from there? What will *become* of us when it overwhelms?

As part of an ever-changing life landscape, it intrigues me that *becoming* is verb, noun, and adjective. As a verb it indicates transition, as a noun it means the process of coming to be something or of passing into a state, and as an adjective, *becoming* describes a person with attractive qualities.

These stories reflect the progress of ideas and action worked through to rebuild a solid life foundation with attractive qualities. Each story or poem bears fruit of that process of sifting through the rubble of life beliefs and unmet expectations. These stories do not follow an exact chronological order, as it often requires more than one sifting through for new concepts to truly take hold.

I am amazed at the power my choices have to move my life story in the direction I want it to head. Although I would never wish tragedy on another person, the *becoming* journey has proved to be life-giving. I invite you to join me in this rebuilding process, of *becoming* someone renewed, a becoming change.

This is my *becoming*.

Contents

Part One
Becoming at Peace with History   15
    Facing History   16
    Myopic Vision   18
    Circular Becoming   22
    The ID Crisis   25
    Searching for Self   28
    Do the Math   29
    Shedding the Old Skin   30

Part Two
Where the Journey Takes Us   33
    Lessons from Down Under and Beyond   34
    Shooting Raw by Default   34
    Roland   38
    Amanda   42
    Mark   45
    Bitter Coffee and a Plastic Rose   47
    The Sound of My Own Voice   51

Part Three
Becoming Educated   59
    She Has a PhD   60
    Lessons from the Slopes   63
    Lessons From The Lanes   66
    Joy Snatchers   68
    Innocent Violations   70
    Closing the Gap   71
    Pat Answers   75

Part Four
Seasons of the Soul   77
    Seasonally Affected   78
    Soul Seasons   80
    The Advent-ure Begins with Hope   82
    Peace of Mind Advent-ure   84
    The Advent-ure of Joy and SAD   86
    Love of Advent-ure   89
    The Easter Sting   92
    The Easter Hallelujah   94
    Pushing through Thick and Thin   96

Part Five
Becoming Open: Helps Along the Way   101
    Chasing the Light   102
    The Call of Beauty   105
    Kayak Moon Chasing   107
    Conversations with I AM   110

Part Six
Stumbling Towards Grace and Resolution   113
    Footwear for the Journey ...   113
    Victory Redefined   114
    My Choice   117
    Moniker Matters ... What's in a name?   118
    Home is Where you Hang your Heart ...   123
    Ride the Moving Wave   128
    Rebuilding Walls   130
    Let me Bloom   137

Epilogue   138
Recommended Books   141
About the Author   143

in the Becoming ...

Part One

History, despite its wrenching pain, cannot be unlived, but if faced with courage, need not be lived again.
                                             Maya Angelou

Becoming at Peace with History

Once upon a time ...

There was a young woman
   who lived in a shoe
with a husband and three children
They knew what to do
They lived, they loved, they danced, and they laughed.
And then just like that
   the shoe collapsed

      the fairy tale ending ... disappeared.

Facing History

If only hindsight were given ahead of time.

Over twenty years ago at a Sunday School teachers' conference, the keynote speaker shared thoughts from her mother's funeral. Seeing her mother in the casket she said, "Finally Mom, your struggling can cease." Her mother had experienced a lifetime of questions and self-doubts, and now in death appeared at peace.

When I was eighteen with a high school diploma in hand and a starry future ahead of me, I felt that I could conquer the world. Buoyed by the confidence that came from growing up a small-town girl at the top of the class, I thought I knew a lot. In my twenties I realized the world was a much bigger place, and after some travel, I saw that I was a small player in a very big world. But I still had ideals into my thirties and thought that by forty I might have it all together, whatever I thought that meant. The forties turned into another decade of transition; those children I'd birthed earlier were becoming adults themselves. As I recognized pieces of myself in them, I laughed at how little I had known at that age, and how it would take a lifetime to figure out this thing we call *life*. It has always been easy to solve world problems from the armchair of a theoretical stance, over a coffee with like-minded people. How many times the world has been saved over lattes?

At the end of my forties, I was becoming more of who I wanted to be, and I could see that the world was expanding and that there was more to life than what had been tasted thus far. At my fiftieth birthday party, I announced that I had lived too much of my life with a sense of cautious optimism, as though waiting for the sky to fall in, and in front of that supportive group I released that caution, intending to live full and free from then on. I declared that God had proved trustworthy; and why should I doubt?

Twenty-two days after that declaration ... The Accident.

The Accident that took a beautiful daughter, the only son, and a future daughter-in-law.

The Accident that now divided life into my personal version of BC and AD: Before Crisis and After Death.

The Accident that put me at Ground Zero and made me wonder why I had boldly stated that God was trustworthy – maybe if I hadn't said that I wouldn't have been challenged on it.

To say that life forever changed is an understatement.

Everything shifted in major ways. The fallout of the accident continued to change the landscape of my life; the big issues moved into my backyard; loss, death, divorce, relocation, job change, pain and suffering – note there are two *effs* in suffering. No longer a theoretical discussion over beverages, suffering became my new and unwanted life.

The mind demanded answers; the heart longed for a return to the simpler before-crisis-life. The quest for true meaning, purpose, understanding and identity was thrown into a sea of pain I had never known possible.

Becoming by choice. Wrestling with the voices. *Becoming* the question of all that did not add up in life.

Myopic Vision

> *Since we cannot change reality, let us change the eyes that see reality.*
>
> Nikos Kazantzakis

Grief afflicts the soul and impairs vision. When your eyesight goes gradually, you don't notice it. As a student in elementary school, I sat in the front row of my classroom whenever possible in order to read the chalk board. There were no mandatory eye tests until I reached junior high, and when I asked my parents about glasses, they thought I wanted them to be cool. We could not afford many extra items, and eyeglasses seemed to fit into that category. It was only when my older sister insisted she needed her eyes examined that an official appointment was made for me as well.

When my glasses arrived my father expressed his utter dismay at their thickness. My mother asked, "Can you really see with those on?" And I expressed my delight – I could see clearly! Now I could sit in the back row if I chose, and I can assure you that I did not choose those cat-eye glasses to be cool. Due to a set of circumstances beyond my control, my vision could not be redeemed without the coke-bottle bottoms.

Before my feet touched the floor in the morning, the glasses were on my face. In high school, thanks again to that same older sister, the miracle of contact lenses became my new mode of vision and I could even see clearly in the cold of winter, when frost would fog the glasses. Contacts also made my first kiss a little easier, no clumsy bumping of glasses askew.

Twenty-five years later, the optometrist said my eyes suffered dryness from overuse of contact lenses. My pursuit of seeing clearly had begun a long time before. LASIK eye surgery was on the rise at the time. I watched the ads, read up on the procedure, prayed, worried, and signed a legal document that indicated I could be blind following the surgery. The doctor also warned that my depth perception could be impacted - and still I went for it.

 I wanted to be sedated. I seriously considered my own self- medication with either drugs or alcohol. The eye surgeon's patronizing laughter did nothing to reduce my anxiety. My husband came along to support me for the procedure and was invited by the surgeon to come into the room and watch. The plan was to operate on both eyes at one time, under local anesthetic. As a nurse with several years of operating room experience, and also assisting with cataract removals, I understood the need for the patient to lie perfectly still to prevent the risk of a blunder. Heroically, I fought my desire to jump off the bed and run out of the room. I lay there thinking they might need to tie me down. I had never been a fan of sitting quietly in the dental chair while the drill burred closer towards my brain, and here I could not close my eyes!

 In fact, they had special eye retractors, left over from some forgotten Second World War torture chamber, to keep my eyes propped open, *wide* open. I was told the procedure took five minutes per eye. Five minutes that were etched in my brain. Five long minutes ... of needing to blink and being unable to.

 The surgeon explained ahead of time that he would drop the freezing into my eye and wait till the eye was frozen before proceeding. I only remember the drop going in, and immediately this machine descended towards my eyeball at the speed of light. In a relaxed jovial manner he directed this laser light show that played out with zips, zaps, and colours in my eyes, which my husband verified were smoking hot. My doctor calmly explained everything to him. He was in awe of the smoke rising from his wife's eyeballs ... and there was I, on the bed, fists clenched tight, counting in my head, reciting peaceful words, wanting to run away ... or shake someone – mainly the two men in the room for laughing at me. What was quick and routine for them felt like an eternity to me. And then my eyes were patched over. After being blinded by the light like Paul in the New Testament, I was led to a recovery room, where I was observed for an hour, then instructed to go home to rest and return the next morning. Dark glasses were provided to cover my eyes at all times. My old glasses were of no use now and the contacts were out of the question. I spent the next sixteen hours laying low, seeing in a foggy haze, and doing nothing that could possibly impact stress levels or pressures in the eyes. I prayed fervently for the operation to work.

The next morning I removed the dressings as per instruction. I can remember the anticipation of the patches coming off. First the right eye, then the left. The tape caught some eyebrow hair as it pulled off, and then the incredible realization –

"I can see, I can see! It's a miracle!" I happy danced about the house, shouting my disbelief.

I sang the Amazing Grace song: "T'was blind, but now I see!" For the next week I wore plastic goggles at night, to reduce the risk of accidental rubs or bumps to my eyes. Eye drops were instilled four times a day to each eye for the first ten days. Two weeks later I returned for the follow-up visit, received confirmation of the surgery's success and away I went.

Many years later, I still marvel at the miracle of the gift of vision. John O'Donohue writes, "The heart of vision is shaped by the state of soul. When the soul is alive to beauty, we begin to see life in a fresh and vital way."

The eyes are the windows to the soul. There is a truth to the adage that once you have seen you cannot unsee. My depth perception has improved, I have *become* aware of a much bigger picture and that picture now includes pain.

Circular Becoming

> *"We shall not cease from exploration, and the end of all our exploring will be to arrive where we started and know the place for the first time."*
>
> T.S. Eliot

For a variety of generational reasons, I accepted the notion early in life that time spent focused on getting to know myself was selfish, that my hours were better spent in the service of others. With many others I frequently sang the song line: *Let's forget about ourselves and concentrate on Him and worship Him.** Did scripture ever suggest that I spend time gazing inward? As a mother of three young children it was easy to forget about myself; in fact, my one spoken desire at the time was to go to the bathroom solo. (I had fairly low standards.) Some small voice or hand always pounded the door in great need. I was well practiced and trained in the art of forgetting about myself. As a nurse, I remember a dual incident of particular trauma that triggered one of the only debrief sessions in my early career (a surgical death and a critical event with a newborn). We were told that self-care was important for us to prevent burnout – this came across as a novel idea. Some unspoken and superior faith-like sacrificial attitude reminded me that I wasn't in need of self-care. The Super-Mom and impossible Proverbs 31 woman was who I should strive to be. Rising early in the morning, feeding households, laughing in the face of winter. We were shamed into relentless service at work and at home with minimal pee or tea breaks. *What were we thinking?* Currently the pendulum has swung heavily to the side of self-care/awareness. Somewhere, there must be a balance of life between the exhaustive giving of oneself and re-energizing self to do so.

Now I have come to realize that while soul care is a vital part of self-care, it is not an interchangeable concept and it requires more diligence than self-care does. While a day at the spa might relieve my immediate anxieties, it might not address my soul needs. If I believe my identity as that of a created daughter of a loving heavenly father, I think I could travel through life feeling more secure, more confident, more loved. Doubts of that daughter identity fuel the notion that getting to know myself is not a valuable use of time. I'm still learning how essential my soul care is; I'm learning that nurturing my soul helps me take better care of myself as well.

On my 57th birthday, I began reading a book called *The Gift of Being Yourself* by David Benner, subtitled *The sacred call to self-discovery*. Was this really a *sacred* call? *Hallelujah!* I thought. *If this was labelled sacred, it could be justified.* I still felt the need to justify the time spent on a self-discovery endeavour. I began on my 57th birthday, after swimming fifty-seven lengths at the pool. It was high time to discover who I was now. The journey which had begun after the accident continued.

I recall holding my sister's ten-day-old grandson. He was so squishable, I could fold his nine pounds of arms and legs into a little football shape. Following the birth of each of my three children, I was amazed that one small embodied life could be squished and released in the birthing process. Ejected from the womb, thrust into life, there was no way for that baby to return to the prenatal chamber. The forces of nature that propelled it out refused its re-entry. John O'Donohue speaks of the butterfly's metamorphosis as a significant visual of the journey of *becoming*. I agree with him when he expresses the idea that once you have crossed certain barriers (birth or death) or gone through a process you cannot go back. Once you have *become* the winged creature of beauty, you cannot go back to being a caterpillar.

Sadly some people die in their cocoons. Unlike the butterfly, we are the caterpillars that have a say in our transformation. Once we've moved out, while impossible for us to return to the cocoon, it is still possible to take two steps forward and one back. Logistically, in the grieving and in the *becoming*, I can only move forward or remain stuck. I cannot go back, because back isn't there anymore. There is both sadness and excitement in this knowing. Often I feel I have one foot in the cocoon and one foot in the air, trying to maintain balance. At these moments it is imperative that I choose to move forward. It is imperative for me to examine my past, both its beauty and its pain, and knead the elements of hope and resiliency into the bread of tomorrow in order to move ahead.

*Bruce Ballinger, "We have Come into His House," © 1976 Sound III, Inc. and MCA Music Publ., A.D.O. Universal Studio.

The ID Crisis

> *You either walk inside your story and own it or you stand outside your story and hustle for your worthiness.*
>
> Brené Brown

With "Silent Night" as background music, mugs of steaming coffee and tea to fight off the December cold, conversation swirled around the dining room table. The question every grade twelve student faced the entire final year came up for my daughter, "So what will you do next year?"

Brittany had planned for Kaléo, what her parents called a travel adventure program, with enough Biblical studies and the odd university credit thrown in to allow for parental support. Whether it was the tall ships sailing off the West Coast or the Vancouver Island location, this program had appeal for my ready-to-explore-life girl. Her same-age cousin at the Christmas table was applying to colleges and universities as was expected of her, a child of two professionals. Lauren sighed and said, "I wish I had a year to spend finding myself."

How often I have thought of her expressed longing – *I wish I had time to spend finding myself* – and here I was in Australia six years later, feeling the need to do exactly that, to find myself. Who was I? How had I *become* so lost? What did it mean to be lost, and what to make of Christ's paradoxical words that only in losing ourselves do we find out who we are? Fifty-four years old with a major identity crisis in a foreign land presented a huge challenge for me. Was it that I had been through the tsunami? My own personal tsunami happened two months after the major Indian Ocean waves of devastation of December 2004. Tragic circumstances changed my landscape and fueled my relocation. This began a search to find out – who was I? Who would I *become* at this stage in life, given my circumstances?

At this stage I was four years post-accident – the accident that took that same Kaléo daughter and her brother on icy roads that cruel winter night. Now those parents and the oldest sister were left to sort and live out the tangled mess, in the aftermath of tragedy. In his book, *A Grace Disguised*, Jerry Sittser nailed it for me when he said:

> Catastrophic loss is like undergoing an amputation of our identity. It is not like the literal amputation of a limb. Rather it is more like the amputation of the self from the self. But it is not simply the loss of identity that causes the problem. It is also the difficult conditions under which a new identity must be formed. One cannot escape it simply by finding a new spouse, a new job, a new life.

It's not easy to just sort out the mess and move on. Each step in the process is done under conditions that were not known before. Peterson's introduction to the book of Malachi in *The Message* says it so well:

> Most of life is not lived in crisis – which is a good thing. Not many of us would be able to sustain a life of perpetual pain or loss or ecstasy or challenge. But crisis has this to say for it: In time of crisis everything, absolutely everything, is important and significant.

Life itself is on the line. No word is casual, no action marginal. And almost always, God and our relationship with God is on the front page. But during the humdrum times, when things are as we tend to say "normal," our interest in God is crowded to the margins of our lives and we become preoccupied with ourselves. Religion during such times is trivialized into asking "God-questions" – calling God into question or complaining about him, treating the worship of God as mere hobby or diversion, managing our personal affairs for our own convenience and disregarding what God has to say about them. Going about our usual activities as if God were not involved in such dailiness.

And so began the next phase of a difficult journey; a journey that moved from survival mode to one of healing, of doubting, of holding on and letting go and being let go. And would that free-floating woman survive? What were the anchors that held her? What would *become* of her?

Searching for Self

In all of creation, identity is a challenge only for humans. A tulip knows exactly what it is. It is never tempted by false ways of being. Nor does it face complicated decisions in the process of becoming. So it is with dogs, rocks, trees, stars, amoebas, electrons and all other things. ... Humans, however, encounter a more challenging existence. We think. We consider options. We decide. We act. We doubt. Simple being is tremendously difficult to achieve and fully authentic being is extremely rare.

David Benner

Who am I? This or the Other?
Am I one person to-day and to-morrow another?
Am I both at once? A hypocrite before others,
And before myself a contemptible woebegone weakling?
Or is something within me like a beaten army
Fleeing in disorder from victory already achieved?

Who am I? They mock me, these lonely questions of mine,
Whoever I am, Thou Knowest, O God, I am thine."

Dietrich Bonhoeffer, "Who Am I?"
in Letters and Papers from Prison

Do the Math

"I am whole and holy,"
    she said.
Not a reduction
More than a half

A fraction of her former self
But larger than she used to be.
Once a fifth of the circle
    and now
Alone in body
But whole in spirit
    Complete.

She never understood the math that well,
But knows that the sum of her parts
    is greater than the division.
Rising with grace in her steps and
Eternity in her eye
    She squares the equation.

Shedding the Old Skin

Everyone tells a story about themselves inside their own head. Always. All the time. That story makes you what you are. We build ourselves out of that story.

Patrick Rothfuss

My grandchildren live in North Africa, in a country with French as the second language after Arabic. Minimal English is spoken in their Muslim neighbourhood. I spent several weeks there one December. My eight-year-old granddaughter rose grumpily for an 8:00 am start at a local private school. Do not think Western style private school. The reason my granddaughter was excited about this school was because this one had real washrooms, not a converted house bathroom that still housed a bathtub. There were two separate rooms; one with four girls' stalls and one with four boys' stalls.

It was with great fanfare and delight that I initiated a doubles ride on the single speed bicycle as a way of getting her to school fairly quickly, something very important for an eight-year-old who dawdled efficiently. "We are rocking the hood," I said to her, as we pedalled the sandy partially paved street, dodging large stones and garbage. She perched on the mounted rear rack, keeping her feet slightly apart holding on to my seat with as firm a grip as eight-year-old fingers could. Like clockwork, our traveling bicycle circus passed the local high school at break time, forcing us to navigate at least two hundred students crossing the street. The head-scarved girls were thrilled to say a *bonjour*, presuming I must be French. I responded to a few of the greetings with a smile and either *Allo* or *bonjour*.

Some of the boys made comments and my granddaughter said "Grandma they're making fun of us, let's just get out of here." As I could not understand the Arabic comments, and saw only smiles and laughter in eyes, I didn't think they were mocking us. I was a novelty in the monolithic landscape, this mature blonde woman with red streaks in my hair. I couldn't be a grandmother, for grandmothers would be fully covered in their long *djellabas*, and never on a bicycle.

"Don't worry Maisha," I said, "they're not being unkind. They're just not comfortable in their own skin."

"I don't get it. You're not a snake, grandma, you don't shed your skin. What do you mean?"

"Sometimes people aren't comfortable with who they are, and then they have to make fun of other people, to feel better. If you feel okay about who you are, you don't have to shed your skin or make fun of other people."

Ah, my dear granddaughter, perhaps shedding some of the old skin is exactly what is needed to *become* who you and I want to be.

Part Two

Sometime in your life you will go on a journey. It will be the longest journey you have ever taken. It is the journey to find yourself.

Katherine Sharp

Where the Journey Takes Us

There is a sixty-year woman
      who wears a new shoe
She decides some things she still wants to do
She laughs and she dances
She takes some bold chances
To become someone new.

Lessons from Down Under and Beyond

I am not the same, having seen the moon shine on the other side of the world.

Mary Anne Radmacher

Shooting Raw by Default

Life is like a camera. Focus on what's important, capture the good times, develop from the negatives and if things don't work out take another shot.

Unknown

My first DSLR camera is purchased a few weeks before a major trip to Israel, Turkey, and Morocco. Three sisters meet from three different countries to travel, laugh and dance our way across our dream destinations. I have a month to experiment with my new camera. After a short briefing by the skinny, blue-jeaned sales guy, I take the Nikon D home with me, but the instruction manual is missing.

They e-mail it to me later; however, I learn better when I can underline commands, even better when I read them, best when I follow them. Recently, I have become quite passionate about photography, although not passionate enough to understand apertures, light exposures, or to read the four photography books taking up space on my shelf. If you buy a nice camera, you can cheat your way into some amazing photographs without reading the books. My cameras and computers have been the class professors on the importance of default positions. My computer has a mind of its own, reformatting itself when I hit an incorrect key. The computer and I have an on-going love-hate relationship. We are working to improve that. With camera experimentation I find that shooting on automatic gives some great shots.

I take pictures in mass quantities, but as we sisters travel, I cannot understand why my camera gobbles up the SD cards like snack food. In every country I search out a camera shop to buy another SD card. Finally, arriving at our last destination, my daughter's place in North Africa, my son-in-law Kevin asks me what resolution I use to shoot my pictures. I don't know. We discover that the skinny, blue-jeaned boy in the camera store had set my DSLR to shoot at *raw* – the highest resolution possible. While the pictures are incredibly vivid, I can only store a fraction of pictures on the SD card compared to the number at a more conventional setting. To shoot *raw* was set as a default in the camera store. I didn't understand that I could change this. I didn't understand it was there to begin with.

Merriam-Webster's online dictionary defines *default* as a verb: "to automatically use a particular setting, option, etc.," and as a noun, "a selection made usually automatically or without active consideration due to lack of a viable alternative." Many of our default positions, our values and views that we hold, form in childhood and we carry on with them as our internal system, unaware that we can change. It can be as simple as my daily response to smaller challenges: do I seek comfort food, go out for a walk, process or ignore and hope things will get better? On a bigger scale, I see the default position as that core statement of my operating system. What carries me through when life becomes unbearable ... unliveable? What is it that I need to hold onto for all I've got, because it is all I've got? Is there a greater power? Is it God or is it myself, a combination? Eugene Peterson has said that when life is normal these issues of God are sidelined, debated in theory, but in tragedy they become the front page.

As an eight-year-old, I set a fundamental default position when I chose to believe that God existed – a desperate plea from a little girl with an alcoholic father: *God, please help me.* Later in the process of grief, I entered the battlefield to determine if I could continue to trust a God I wasn't sure was still trustworthy, but the alternative of life without God loomed even more fearful for me.

Tragedy made me aware of the importance of my default positions. My camera taught me that I could change the settings. This has been huge for me to realize, first to see that these settings exist in my inner beliefs, and then to understand that I can change these settings. Understanding and changing your own default settings is one of the most liberating and most difficult things to do.

In a previous life I held certain default positions. One was that if you worked hard, lived right, believed in God, then life would be good. Yes there might be some troubles to sort out, but basically life would and should be good. (Reap what you sow idea.)

I believe we come into this world as babies not quite with a blank page, because I also believe we are hardwired for some things. I believe that as a created being I am designed to connect with the eternal, the God of our creation. I believe there is an aching to believe, a longing to be part of a bigger story than our own little lives.

David Benner, in his book *The Gift of Being Yourself*, talks about defaults and addresses a major issue that I was unaware of - the importance of *knowing oneself*. While I'd heard that often, I never understood what it meant. I had bought into the default doctrine that too much time spent focusing on your own identity was selfish and not a worthy pursuit. My focus had been to learn about God, not about myself.

Unaware that these default settings are part of the make-up that forms my identity, it is liberating to discover that, like my camera, I have a say in the choice of the setting. I do not have to shoot on raw, I've had enough of those raw experiences. Let me use the fisheye setting. I want the happy setting. And now it *becomes* a more avant-garde setting.

Roland

> *For now we see through a glass, darkly, but then face to face. Now I know in part; but then shall I know, even as also I am known.*
>
> 1 Corinthians 13:12 KJV

People-watching is a hobby of mine. As people pass by the window of the burger bar, I decide to do a mini survey on the number of people talking or texting as they walk. Several yesses in a row pass by. This venue is ideal, with raised bar stools facing the street, where lone customers can sit and not feel isolated. From my elevated perch on a major downtown street of Perth, Australia I observe a microcosm of life passing by – old, young, confident, unsure, dodgy, groups, well and poorly dressed individuals, those deep in thought, those with no apparent thoughts.

And then I see him. He stands out from the steady stream. His gait, affected by cerebral palsy, has him pushing one of those senior style walkers with a seat and wire-framed shopping basket. He makes his way to the bus stop, puts his dark face close to the pole and studies the bus time tables. Several people are already in line. He shuffles from side to side away from the queue and takes up residence right in front of me. His Spanish-style black felt hat does not quite cover ear-length, grey-tinged black hair, giving him a strong South American look. A well-worn grey overcoat covers his faded white shirt and greyed tie beneath – a well-used, infrequently-laundered set of Sunday clothes. My eyes fixate on him, wondering what his life might be like. More than the fast-food pane of glass separates us. As Bus 102 comes into view he stands, slowly rushing to the line with hurry in his eye and ineloquent feet dragging.

Six able-bodied people quickly get on board. A young couple just ahead of him stands on the running board asking the driver for directions, appear to change their minds and get off the bus. Mr. Latino moves his walker forward to board but the unthinkable happens: the doors close. The bus departs just as he tries to get on. Utter frustration, mingled with anger and disbelief, crosses his face as he pounds his fist onto his walker bars. Then, with a look of acceptance and drooped shoulders, he makes his way back to the spot in front of me. The bus lumbers away without him and tears come to my eyes as I think about all the little difficulties and setbacks he must face regularly because of his condition. I think of my sister who works to improve quality of life and accessibility for people living with disabilities. At that moment I am incredibly thankful for what she is doing. I am also mindful of another sister who lives with the effects of MS on her body – a body that does not obey her mind when she tells it to walk. I remember the exhaustion I witnessed in the eyes of a mother of an autistic teenage patient a few years ago. Her son needed a general anesthetic in order to have the dentist look into his mouth, clean and fix his teeth. *The glass window separates us profoundly.* I wonder if there is anything that I can do?

Perhaps little, but I make up my mind not to let the bus miss this man again. I am down to the chocolate sundae of my four-piece meal deal, which has lost its appeal after witnessing this injustice. In ways that this man does not understand, I connect with him. My own grief has given me an invisible yet disabling affliction to live with as well. I drop my wrappers in the garbage, go outside and start a conversation.

"I saw what just happened there."

He looks up with resignation. "I was just waiting politely in the queue when the couple got off. I guess the bus driver didn't see me. It often happens." He does not express anger. I ask when the next bus will come. "A half an hour."

"Well I know I can't change what happened, but could I at least pay for your bus fare?"

"Oh, no, but thanks." He refuses a second payment offer. I stay and chat until his bus arrives. The usual questions follow: Where are you from? What do you do? He has a social sciences degree and is now doing freelance journalism. "Being at home makes it easier to work," he tells me. "Getting out and about is a challenge." He sounds matter of fact about his situation.

Thirty-five years ago, as a child, he immigrated with his family from India via Uganda. On this day he has come from the beautiful St Mary's Cathedral, which has recently undergone a million-dollar renovation. He expresses uncertainty, with many pressing needs in the world. "It is a beautiful building and will be around for a long time, but I'm not sure the cost is justified." I presume his faith base might be Catholic. From a generic, non-personal stance we discuss some of the forms of religion. He then asks about my life situation and what brought me to Australia. I speak of my eldest daughter and he asks if I have other children.

"I lost a son in a car accident." It seems safe to presume he does not have children.

"How long ago? ... That must have been hard." The pause in the air, when neither party knows how much further to pursue the conversation. "What caused the accident? Was he speeding?"

"Icy roads," I say. "We have bad weather conditions. He was not even driving. His girlfriend was. She was also killed. We should have been planning a wedding, but instead we had a funeral." He is silent and I realize for *my* sake I cannot even tell him that my youngest daughter had also been in that car.

For those who have lost someone dear, it is extremely painful to put this loss into mere words, and this conversation is not about me trying to let him know I have experienced challenges as well. Pain and suffering have a way of connecting people, as though the glass barrier *becomes* permeable. I do not need a walker the way he does, but I do need to hold a heavenly hand for constant support. Strange, I had not intended this conversation to focus on me, just as he did not want the conversation to focus on him and his difficulties. He asked for my email address earlier in the conversation, and I was reluctant to give it to him. As Bus 102 approaches he extends his hand, I return the handshake and give him my email address as well. This time people move out of the way to let him board first. I wave to him through the bus window. My heart slightly heavier, I pedal home in the paradise sunshine of the day, but there is also a sense of gratitude in my heart, a sense of connection with humanity, a sense of *becoming* open to the light that shines through the glass.

Amanda

> *If any one of you is without sin, let him be the first to throw a stone at her.*
>
> John 8:7, NIV

I first take note of her in the minuscule coffee room, where strangers, co-workers, salespeople, drug addicts, university students, researchers, doctors, nurses, and the occasional cockroach under the sink congregate on a daily basis. I wonder if anyone can come in off the street to have coffee at the Drug Treatment Clinic. Her cabaret-style black fedora is the first thing I notice, and then the shapely legs below the barely-covering jet-black shorts, and a form-fitted, off-one-shoulder, cleavage-revealing black sweater. You can say she stands out from the usual coffee crowd. Her confident look speaks of someone who belongs here, someone comfortable in her skin and someone familiar with being in charge. Questions run through my mind as to which people group category she belongs to. I decide not to know or to ask, and I thank her for heating up the kettle as I steal water from the boiling jug before she can fill her waiting coffee cup. No response and I quickly depart with my tea for the *doctah*. They are still archaic enough to feel that the *doctahs* should have their tea made and delivered. I don't mind doing it for Dr. John. Two procedures later, I am ready to call for our next client. When I call "Amanda?" I am surprised that the black fedora follows me into the humble treatment room.

At the drug clinic we do a marvellous little procedure: we implant slow release time capsules that contain a blocker drug. Under local anesthetic, this implant which reduces the addict's cravings, is inserted beneath the fatty tissues of the lower abdomen. We administer antibiotics to reduce the risk of infection as our clientele's lifestyles often compromise their immune systems. Prescribed antibiotics are routine to prevent the huge set-back an infection brings. As Dr. John begins the explanation, Amanda interrupts. She knows her stuff. She questions the necessity of antibiotics, as they cause thrush to such an extent that she needs expensive treatment for it. If we do give her antibiotics, she asks, can we also give her a prescription for the thrush medication as they cost minimum $20 a pill, and she will need up to ten days of them. We discuss the possibility of only one dose of antibiotics. I check with the other doctor about the second medication, and I am told it is available over the counter.

Amanda is aware of this, but she also knows that if it is prescribed for her, she does not have to pay for it. "I can't afford it," she tells me. Her clinical notes indicate that she has been spending up to $250 per day for heroin. I do the math, and I think, *This is brilliant.* Similar reasoning as the smokers who say they cannot afford milk for the children while supporting their pack a day habit. I use the same judgement and logic here. In a patronizing voice, I suggest to her that as she was supporting a $250 a day habit until forty-eight hours ago, she could probably afford the treatment if she gets thrush.

She turns to look me square in the eye, and without a flinch declares, "But I'm not a prostitute anymore."

My mouth remains silent and my inside-jaw drops, as does Doctor John's. *Cha-ching* – a point for the lady. We do not suggest that she find the means to pay for the medication. Instead, we decide that one oral dose of antibiotics is the best way to go, and we hope she will not get an infection. As the procedure continues, I sense that both Dr. John and I want to make her feel cared for. We remain silent as she hoists herself onto the treatment bed. She pulls down her shorts before Dr. John can say, "No don't take them off, just lie down and pull them below your belly button."

In the dropping of her shorts, Amanda reveals a lovely floral tattoo that stretches from her right upper thigh to iliac crest. Amanda states, "If you want to get a tattoo, either have your clothing reveal all of it, or none of it." In the past, Dr. John has let me know that he is fundamentally opposed to tattoos; I am still learning to appreciate their artwork.

Dr. John voices the question for both of us, "So what do you wear to fully reveal this tattoo?"

"Very high cut bathers present the whole bouquet."

Following this, we joke with Amanda about the difficulties of having ever-changing partners' names tattooed on the body. She tells us of a lady who has four different men's names tattooed under her breasts, and roses on the full part of the breast, but after three children, she'd aged and … she trails off and I finish for her: "They're all long stem roses now."

"Exactly," she laughs.

I have the inexplicable feeling that I am with Jesus in the presence of the woman who was caught in the very act of adultery, with my hand clutching a stone. It is *becoming* my choice to let the stone drop.

Mark

Scars are tattoos with a better story.

Anonymous

Mark is an earlier client we'd had, age 26, a year younger than my son would've been. Automatically I take note of the patients with the same years of birth as my own children and wonder how similar or dissimilar my kids would be in their lives if they still had them. I wonder silently if that will ever go away. Tears spring to my eyes, I blink hard to make them disappear. As Mark removes his sweater, known as a jumper in Australia, his chest reveals in Gothic print the tattoo *A Thugs Life*. I ask him,

"What is the story of your tattoo?" I am learning that tattoos are significant as a part of a person's identity. It feels sad to me that people too often by age 20 brand themselves for life with labels born out of anger, rebellion or what appears as plain stupidity.

"Yea, it says *A Thugs Life*, something I did a few years ago when I was in a different space," he reluctantly admits. And this was what he aspired to? Thankfully I keep that thought to myself.

"You know the *A* is quite artsy, and I think with the right designer you could turn that into *Hugs 4 Life*. What do you think? That'd be a real turn around." He stumbles into the recovery room without a response, but as I leave him in the care of volunteers and one nurse, I do wish him hugs for life.

Dr. John flashes a mischievous smile as we walk back to the treatment room and suggests that I should go into creative tattoo artistry renovation. "The reason I don't like tattoos is because I spent hours as a plastic surgeon trying to remove those inscriptions made in moments of poor judgement. One should be careful; you might not want to be a thug for the rest of your life." I am learning that compassion is much more *becoming* than judgment.

Bitter Coffee and a Plastic Rose

Sweet is the voice of a sister in the season of sorrow.
                                            Benjamin Disraeli

Garbage litters the streets as we navigate the unmarked roads. What had been urban five minutes ago is now rural, with goats, chickens, and sheep that wander about the brown sand and gravel mix in search of nourishment. Through the palms to the left, the blue water of the Mediterranean is visible. Empty tourist zone hotels await the arrival of warmer weather. Our Peugeot Partner stops at the stucco house and three women step out from the shadowed entranceway. The mother's full-length brown house dress hides her slight frame. Two younger women in tight blue jeans and long shirts stand beside her.

Kisses, two times to each cheek, and greetings of *S'lemma* and *la bess* are exchanged and my daughter Kristen, her friend Nyla, my grandson, and I are welcomed into their home. Threadbare rugs provide cushion from the concrete floor, while a lone bulb from a wired socket lights the hallway as we follow our hosts to the salon room.

Although we have come with a purpose in mind, my daughter lets these women lead in the conversation, which quickly turns to the matter that we have come about. It is an official bereavement visit. I had known that the foreign words would swirl about my head, but I sense where the conversation is going as I observe the sadness and the tears of the mother who is doing most of the talking. Kristen stops occasionally to translate:

"She had just left for school with her sister. They were only a thousand meters from home when the taxi hit her.

It wasn't dark, and they cannot understand how the driver wouldn't have seen her."

More Arabic flows and Nyla's tears collect in the corner of her eyes as the story unfolds. I can see the urgency on the mother's face. She relives the account as she speaks. She strokes her chest over and over; I envision this mother cradling and stroking her fourteen-year-old daughter as she bleeds and loses consciousness. I stroke my grandson who is quietly attentive to the chain around my neck, as if he perceives the sacredness of the moment and is quiet out of respect. I hold my breath as the mother tells us how she held her daughter for almost two hours waiting for the ambulance to arrive.

"The blood has not yet washed off the road," she says. The daughter was transported by air to a larger centre in the capital city eight hours away. Over the next month she faded away, with her mother constantly at her bedside.

Kristen moves to the sister and strokes her hand in comfort as the tears rolled down both sets of cheeks. The mother's voice is now silent. There is little for me to say. "I am so sorry."

That translates into her language. I add, "I too have lost a daughter. It is very difficult."

The mother returns my gaze. "I too am sorry."

Kristen asks to see a photo. The sister leaves the room and returns with a happy image of herself and her sister smiling at a recent wedding, a month before the accident. Two lovely sisters captured in time at the happiest of events. For this family, the days will now be marked as a *before* and *after*. The defining moment when everything changes. I know. And I also know it will get worse. Death is painful, whatever language is spoken.

Later in the vehicle as we drive back to my daughter's house, Nyla tells us, "We need to help this mother forget. We should not speak her daughter's name anymore." The language barrier does not allow further discussion on that concept. I wonder, *for whose sake should the beautiful daughter's name not be spoken?* Is it for the benefit of the survivors, so that they will not feel guilt that their child is alive? Is it so that after a brief period of mourning, all can pretend that life is back to normal? *Normal* is never a part of the bereavement experience, except to create paths towards the *new normal*.

In the salon, the mother continues, "When I go to prepare supper, I miss her the most. She would always come in to tell me how her day had gone, what had happened in school. The day before the accident, she stood looking out the window talking to me. She shivered and said to me, 'Something feels strange.'" The mother pauses and then asks "Did she have a sense of foreboding?" There are no answers. There is no comfort, but connection and understanding drape over us like a warm blanket.

The conversation shifts as my daughter speaks and I know by the looks that she is telling them my story, my loss, which is her story as well, for it was also her only sister, her only brother. All eyes convey sympathy as they look towards me. The respectful silence that follows is interrupted by Houda, the niece who is also in the room. In English she asks if we would like coffee. Kristen declines, saying it is not necessary, but Houda turns to me and repeats the coffee question.

"Coffee would be good."

I may not be able to join in Arabic, but I would like to join the ritual of drinking coffee, cementing the bond that has been created over a shared heart story.

As we prepare to leave after coffee and further conversation, the sister scurries out of the room, and returns with a packaged plastic rose for me, the kind sold to tourists. Humbled with her thoughtful gesture, I accept it.

Bitter coffee and a plastic rose, inadequate compensation for death.

The Sound of My Own Voice

> *Without knowing what I am and why I am here, life is impossible.*
>
> Leo Tolstoy

The first six months in Perth, West Australia, test my survival skills as I transition to the land of didgeridoos. The blue waves of the Indian Ocean draw me in, soothing my soul. Water and sky meet at sunset to the melody of the rainbow lorikeet. The red sandy soil and the buzz of the city are a short train ride apart. I fall in love with my new home. What people see as bravery for moving half a world away is really a sign of desperation on my part for something good to transpire in my life.

The Perth outside of the hospital is perfect, but life in the Operating Room theatres (OR), my full-time workplace, becomes increasingly challenging. As the staff is overrun with new recruits, much of my orientation becomes a self-learning package, with me asking a lot of questions. Eight other newcomers join me in the theatres. Two of the nurses are from West Africa, and I am the Canadian import, an experienced nurse trying out life on another planet. Since I do not know another soul on arrival, I am counting on work connections to fill in the social gap. The Australian English has a drawl that outshines the Texans, turning it into a language of its own. The surgeons have renamed every surgical instrument. When is a hemostat not a hemostat? When it's a *snap* (said very quickly.) Twice during surgery I turn lights off instead of on, as the switches are opposite to what we have in Canada, flipped up for *off* instead of up for *on*. Every day ends in exhaustion after working hard mentally to hear and translate what is said, and then to act quickly.

A key component in OR nursing is finding the right equipment ahead of the needed time. You are trained to anticipate, to prevent problems instead of treating them. Any free time I have is spent on self-directed treasure hunts through the multiple supply rooms where floor to ceiling shelving units bulge with mass quantities of medical stuff, from specialty bandages to suction tubes, to artificial knee components to power tools. While I begin with great enthusiasm, a tiny red flag is raised my first day after I learn that the head nurse of the OR has been let go with very little explanation. She is one of the three who had interviewed me, several months prior. Although I sense staff concern, I am too caught up with my own steep learning curve to comprehend the anxious undercurrents. The hospital has eleven theatres running and the hospital itself has recently been purchased by a larger healthcare organization. Oblivious to the politics, I step into this scenario eager to please, to work hard, to dive headfirst into my new life in Australia. I am a team player, assigned to the wrong team.

About that time my daughter is to give birth to her second child in a country that she has recently moved to with her husband and two-year-old daughter. Prior to my acceptance of the hospital job offer, I arranged to have the needed weeks off to help my daughter at the necessary time. This arrangement was made with the head nurse who is no longer here, and also means I am away for three weeks early in my new position. When I return to work after this trip, I have my three-month evaluation, although

I have not worked for three months. Branwen, my superior in her black suit, tells me that I am *floundering*; they expect more from me. My nursing evaluation does not go as well as I'd hoped. Never in thirty years have I been given a negative job review. Walking home that day I feel stunned, alone and confused. *What have I done, leaving everything to come here for this?* Pressure mounts when I am told by a co-worker that I am being watched.

By default my nature is to believe that criticism must be valid and I shouldered responsibility for each problem. I recall an incident years earlier when I assisted in a gall bladder operation. The surgeon began to close up the wound, when I quietly whispered to him that I did not have the specimen yet. This was a very polite way of saying the gall bladder was still in the patient; the surgeon had not taken it out, even though that was the surgical focus. Here in Australia, I know I am not at the top of my game, but I also know that I do not deserve the negative review.

Over drinks a few days later Noreen, another newcomer, shares that she also received a negative performance review. That day she has an unnerving experience with one of the long-time nurses. Lora, an imposing nurse with a twenty-year history at the hospital, takes great pleasure in making life miserable for the new staff. Noreen is in a bathroom stall when Lora enters the room and starts to complain to the other nurse about all the rookies.

"I just love making it hard for them," Lora says as Noreen finishes her pee.

"I knew I couldn't leave" Noreen tells me. "Can you believe it? I climbed up on the toilet seat so they wouldn't know I was there. I wanted to flush myself down after she said she didn't like the nurse assigned to her that day. That was me. Instead of flushing I waited until Lora left. When it was finally quiet I came out." Pause.

"I am almost 50 years old. My life is too short for this kind of crap." After two glasses of wine, Noreen and I have creative options and responses to our reviews. We plan to dress Branwen in her black high heels, baggy blue scrubs, the required paper hairnet over her well-coiffed reds and send her into the swearing surgeon's room. Let her stand in the line of rapid-fire profanity. He doesn't care who gets his *effing* suction. Life doesn't seem quite as bad after that conversation; I realize it isn't just me. For the most part I can get along well with anyone. I also feel fortunate not to be on Lora's hit list.

A genuine concern I have is that I am sent into *any* operating room, including the cardiac surgery room, which is extremely specialized. The cardiac nurses form their own clique. They don't mingle in the lunchroom. I have no cardiac experience or orientation to this room of nonstop beeping machines where crises erupt in a heartbeat. In those critical moments, everyone needs to know what to do quickly. I speak to the nurse manager about my reluctance to be relief staff without training. The senior nurses are given their sweet spots, their chosen areas of expertise; they aren't assigned to float in and out of all areas. Being the new kid on the block I have no such privilege.

I long for my position back in my home hospital, where I was respected and valued as a team member. This poor review does nothing to bolster my self-confidence or my performance, and I feel that one more area of my life is being taken away. *Am I not a good nurse?* What these people do not know is that I am dealing with my divorce at this time ... not a chance I am going to inform them. (Generally I separate work and personal life fairly well.)

Branwen has about as much caring in her as a jellyfish. She prides herself on the hospital's profitability. This is a privately-run hospital where surgeons buy their OR time. It is important for her to run a tight ship; making money matters. The last straw comes when Branwen informs me that the hospital holds my visa, therefore my permission slip to stay in Australia is technically in her hands. Conversations with two of my sisters convince me that my life is too short to work in this toxic environment. Waves of fear and determination battle within me as I struggle with my workplace dilemma.

I prepare emotionally and mentally for my review follow up. My sisters cheer me on from afar. I have my speech written out. I am not going to be intimidated. I am not going to cry, or crumble over and die. I ask if the Human Resources manager can be present at the meeting. On the much-dreaded day, I finish my work shift early and change for my meeting. I bring a change of clothing so I can dress in office wear as well. Branwen in her little black suit and high heels is not going to make me feel shabby in OR scrubs. I change, put my lipstick on, say a prayer, and march into the room with my shoulders back and my head held high. This day I take my voice back ... I will take responsibility for the things that are my issues; I will not take responsibility for working under hostile conditions and a poor orientation, or to live under the threat of my immigration visa being revoked. Before she or the HR person begin, I speak.

"I would like to say something."

In a very respectful manner and unwavering voice I read my 1219-word letter to the two of them. Closing comments from my speech are as follows:

> In your final comments to me, you spoke of some soul searching that should be done on my part. And you did say "It is in our best interests to keep you here, we know you have the experience we just have to 'suck it out of you.'" I left that evaluation wondering if it was in my best interest to remain. The threat of visa revocation was unbelievable. There is no doubt in my mind I would have reached a good working level within three to four months had I been encouraged instead of criticized. To have a staff member tell me, "You are being watched, they are not happy with you" is quite unnerving. The atmosphere of pointing out others' mistakes to build one's self up is very harsh for newcomers. The sense of being a team for the good of the patient is lacking here. I have since stepped back a bit, and have noted other nurses doing similar things, as in small mistakes – for them it was ok, but for me it was something to report. Do people ever report anything good and if they do, does it get passed on to the nurse? From my perspective I have invested a great deal financially, physically and emotionally to make this move to Australia. Thus far what I have read about the hospital and its "employee value" policy has not met my expectations.

For a brief moment they are silent, and then Branwen is all over me asking what can be done to improve. I think she fears I might bring this concern to the Labour

Board. We agree to meet in two weeks, although I know I am done. This is not the earlier version of myself. While I have a fierce sense of justice when it involves others, I tend to overlook unfairness towards myself and to accept the short end of the stick. This time I stood up for myself and for some of the other newcomers who also have their visas tied to this position. With a very small swagger in my step I walk out of the room, glad and relieved that I met the challenge.

Personal victory does come at a cost though, the cost of my job security and my ability to remain in Australia. What am I going to do next? I know I do not want to return to Canada. More importantly I know that I am not willing to let my soul be sucked out by Branwen and her cohorts.

I am only beginning to see that I am *becoming* someone new ... and I am starting to like her.

Part Three

What we know matters but who we are matters more.
Brené Brown

Becoming Educated

We are not human beings on a spiritual journey,
we are spiritual beings on a human journey.
Stephen Covey

She Has a PhD

> *Education is not preparation for life; education is life itself.*
>
> John Dewey

I could say I have my PhD.

One day at the pool, while getting some paper from the bathroom stall to wipe my nose, the toilet paper holder falls apart. I move the piece down, and then, with authority and force, snap it back together. With admiration in her voice another swimmer says to me, "I see you have your PhD in toilet paper recovery." How wonderful to have my credentials acknowledged.

It feels as though I have been bestowed an unwanted PhD in Grief, from the ancient University of Life, also known as the School of Hard Knocks. To be sure this PhD (*Personally have Done it*) is more difficult to obtain, and the thesis more challenging to write, than if I had only done armchair research. I'm not sure if I graduated *cum laude* – does anyone offer praise for these life lessons? The Grace and Forgiveness major was forced upon me. This PhD is mostly experiential; the reading list follows the hands-on program, usually a self-directed list, better known as a survival kit. The interesting thing is that it has a very unregimented, personalized format, with an unspecified length of time for credit completion. An outline is never given or followed and to no surprise it links closely to your own life circumstances. Not only does it take on a life of its own, it nearly owns that life for the duration of the course, and it carries on with no graduation date in sight.

Courses for the Divinity Outlook program are not optional:

1. Forgive God
   (This comes across as arrogant but feels like a requirement.)
2. Forgive Yourself: Don't Be Hard on Yourself
3. Forgive Everyone Else
   (Yes, this is impossible but go ahead and try.)
4. Travel through Thick and Thin
5. See Through a Glass Dimly
6. How to Clean Glasses
7. Fifty Shades of Lemonade: How to Make Your Own to Share
8. Graciousness with Unwanted Advice: Practical Tips for Pasting on a Smile
9. Tripping Over Cliches: When Pat Answers, She Misunderstood the Question
10. Armchair Tragedy: When Others Compare Their Chair Story to Your Real Life
11. Learning to Trust and Live Again
    (This course requires frequent re- certification.)

The forgiveness courses are similar to having teeth pulled without anesthetic. Although pain threshold varies greatly from person to person, most students do not opt for that. Some core basics are required for all courses and workshops. Some instructors have lower expectations and equal experience, and they offer workshop sessions, one-hour introductory courses, or a Sunday morning church lecture. As these instructors develop and age, they will probably go back to revise their lectures or offer a refund on their classes. Support and study groups pop up spontaneously. People in this course find one another, which makes the gripe sessions more bearable and helps build bonds with a variety of people from differing walks of life. At the completion of any course, you do not get a nice certificate to hang on the wall, fortunately. People land in these programs unexpectedly, with little preparation.

I have *become* aware that the older I get, the less I know with certainty, and that beauty shines bright through those faces on course.

Lessons from the Slopes

> *Much of the stress and emptiness that haunts us can be traced back to our lack of attention to beauty. Internally, the mind becomes coarse and dull if it remains unvisited by images and thoughts which hold the radiance of beauty.*
>
> John O'Donohue

The sun is shining, the snow inviting, the air crisp and clean. I don't have time for this, but I also know that I don't not have time for this. Ideas and deadlines swirl in my mind. The publication date for my first memoir is near and weighs heavy. I've tried to make bargains with God along the way, and now as the date approaches, I question myself again. *What am I thinking to let so many people in on my personal grief journey? How will this all play out?* I am afraid.

Fifty-five minutes to the west, the Rocky Mountains invite me to come play for the day. Skis, poles, mitts, goggles, boots, I mentally check off the list as each item is placed in the back of my Rav4. Coffee in hand, I head west into the majesty and grandeur of the snowy peaks. As I round the first curve, I can feel my soul lift, my worries shrink, and my frame lighten by five pounds. One of the attractions for my recent move to live in this area was to reconnect with the freedom found on the ski slopes. While Mount Norquay near Banff has steep runs that ice quickly on a sunny day, it offers proximity and the best lift ticket prices in the area.

This morning the chair lift lurches me twenty feet above ground as my skis hang heavy from boots and swing in the air. I breathe deep as the snowboarders lift and jump below me. The beauty of skiing is that the over-busy mind is forced to focus in order to manoeuvre the two skinny pieces of fibreglass beneath one's feet. This day, as I reach the top of the mountain, I see the Valley of Ten Peaks to my right, pristine snowy beauty all around.

The panoramic picture is suddenly too big, too high. All this grandeur and here is little old me. I feel that recurring fear, the dryness of mouth, the slight shortness of breath. What was I thinking getting on this lift? I must be crazy. Now I'm at the top of this mountain, and somehow I have to get down. I don't think I can do this. I will never be a writer or a skier. Both prospects overwhelm me. My legs don't want to move. I don't know how I will get down. I suppose I can slide. I don't want to get hurt.

In that instant I am carried back to the time I first learned to ski in the mountains, feeling that same leg-paralyzing terror and the throat-choking fear, because I could not see ahead of me. All I could see was that the mountain dropped away and I felt certain that I would fall off the edge into oblivion. At that time, my friend Al, who was instructing me, came alongside and said, "Jocelyn, the mountain will unfold." He instructed me to ski until the edge, to stop, and then to look for the next way down. The mountain would unfold as I went, one segment at a time.

The memory of Al's encouragement puts newfound strength into my legs as I take a deep breath and start to move my skis. As I reach each edge, I discover there is a way down, to the next drop and the next, one section at a time. Even though I am skiing solo, it's as though an unseen guide's reassuring voice says, *Trust me. It's a process. You can do it, one stretch at a time.* I do not get chair-lifted down the mountain. No, I still need to ski, but as I glide, I catch my breath, appreciating the snowy beauty, the sense of freedom, and the rejuvenating presence of the Spirit. At the bottom I hesitate momentarily before getting right back onto that creaky chairlift again ... and again. By the end of the day I am physically done, but emotionally rejuvenated, ready to face the next stretch. Too often my uncertainty of the future strangles my hope for this day.

    I do not want to live a timid life of fear. Scripturally, I've been told to say to the mountain, "Move," and it will, but I know the Rockies are staying. I am learning to *become* more trusting of the Spirit to unfold the mountains before me.

Lessons From The Lanes

Feeling beautiful has nothing to do with what you look like.
Emma Watson

I am a swimmer. In addition to the odd navel lint, I've picked up many life lessons in the pool, such as: Fat and water don't mix – fat floats, therefore all body sizes can enjoy the water. If you want to feed your insecurities, stand naked in the pool shower; but if you want to feel okay about yourself, also stand naked in the pool shower – there are endless body shapes and sizes. The pool offers an on-going lesson in how to get over yourself. You can also shower in your swimsuit. Some mornings when I swim, the pool lanes are labelled Slow, Medium, Fast. With only four lanes, I choose Medium or Slow. But, after the triathletes vacate their fast lane, I choose it, and discreetly nudge the Fast sign to the edge of the adjoining lane.

This morning as I join someone already in the lane she says, "I'm not that strong a swimmer, I do some swimming and some jogging back and forth."

"Whatever works," I reply.

She jogs on and I front crawl past her. I wonder why she told me that. Half-way down the lane, I realized that she was apologizing for herself. She was exercising in lane swim hour, but not doing the standard swim strokes. How many times had I felt out of place when I started at the pool? People would lap me, again and again. What was I doing acting as though I was a swimmer, sharing the same water as triathletes? When I'm alone in the lane I feel no pressure, but when there are two or three swimmers per lane, I feel the need to apologize each time my arm or leg bumps into another swimmer, even if it's their fault ... *so sorry to be in your space.*

I stop at the end of the lane, lift my goggles from my eyes. I am not in this for their sakes, I am in the pool for my sake. We all have the right to be here, and the sooner I stop comparing myself to others the more buoyant I *become.*

One morning a group of Grade One students arrives after my weekly aquasize class is done. Most of the aquasize ladies are in their late sixties or seventies with real grandma bodies, soft and comfortable for hugs, with a little extra pudding. It is freeing to be with this group of women who are comfortable with their bodies and peculiar vein-coloured appendages. This morning the six-year old girls chatter non-stop while getting their swimsuits on. Their chatter continues as they start towards the pool. You have to walk past the showers to get to the pool. As they round the corner, the girls go dead silent. Their mouths stop mid-word in a big open circle. They cannot take their eyes off the *nakeds* in the shower.

Each wave of girls repeats the sequence of chatter, silence, eyes wide-open, fixating on the marshmallow ladies. Somehow I think this is not the picture of grandma that they envision. The grannies have their own outbursts of laughter following the phys ed class walk-through.

One stroke of pool luck: I have found a solution for my increasing facial wrinkle count. This morning as I struggle to get a swim cap on – yes, I wear a swim cap to keep my ear plugs in and the water out of my ears – as I pull this girdle-like-cap on my head, I feel it sucking my scalp upwards. I smile as my skin pulls up and back. A face lift without surgery. *Hmmm,* I wonder. *Does my swim cap go with my little black dress?*

Joy Snatchers

The robbed that smiles, steals something from the thief.
                                William Shakespeare

This is now my fifth time in Morocco; I have grown accustomed to jostling for my space alongside donkeys, djellaba-clad women, and school children racing through the narrow cobblestone streets of the ancient Medina. We exit the five-hundred-year-old city walls, leaving the claustrophobic tightness behind; spacious grasses flourish for grazing sheep and yellow flowers polka-dot the green. My daughter and I ascend the well-worn rock steps to the Marinids tomb of the kings. No one is in sight, although I note one young man cutting a diagonal path below me to the left, and a flock of sheep on my right. So I'm surprised to feel someone bump up against me. I turn only to realize that this same young man is now eye-to-eye in my space. The bump turns into a forceful tug as he tries to grab my shoulder bag from me. Stunned, I scream. My daughter, a few steps above me, spins around to see her mother being thrown to the ground. She shouts at this man in Arabic, *Hashooma! Hashooma!* (Shame on you! Shame on you!) as she quickly descends the few steps that separate us. The young man turns and flees empty handed.

"Mom, are you ok? Are you ok?"

"Well I've never had that happen to me before, and I was not going to let that bugger get a hold of my bag." *Did I really say bugger?* I think I did. I'm surprised that's the only thing I said! The flock of sheep come closer with the shepherd now in sight. Kristen and I sit there, in shocked silence. A group of three women appear below us and call up to ask if we are all right, they'd heard the noise. My daughter explains what happened and they apologize to us, as if they were responsible.

It is broad daylight, the middle of the afternoon. What a brazen attack. I dust off my pants, noting my quite scuffed right shoe. On each of my past visits to this city, I've come alone to this same spot to walk in the early morning. At least twice, a Berber man selling his wares warned me, in fairly good English, that I should not walk here by myself, that this is a dangerous place. The one time I bought three hats from him. In my naivete, I continued to walk there. I had even walked on the far side, hidden from the view of the road. The beauty had beckoned me, and his warnings about "people who do hashish there" fell on my deaf ears.

This bright afternoon the sheep *baa* as they should and I feel a huge relief that I've never been accosted while alone. I am reminded of the verses where Jesus talks about being the good shepherd, the one who lays down his life for the sheep. This thief tried to steal my purse, but he didn't know the treasures I have in there. More important than my credit cards or cash is my late daughter's New Testament. That book symbolizes a hope I share with my daughter even in her death and the bag itself had also belonged to her. How quickly things can change, however watchful we must be. I am thankful to have kept these treasures, thankful that we are alright.

This day I am given a new image of joy snatchers.

Innocent Violations

A day, brims with innocence and beauty,
Two women walk in foreign lands.
A tug at her shoulder turns to a pulling,
A ripping, a violation,
From deep within a scream
As eye to eye, brief moment,
Etches a snapshot of his face.
Thrown to the ground, treasure held tight,
She will not be beat into submission,
The rage of past and future violations
give strength and fury to the fight.
Sister-daughter-friend spins round to help
Hashooma! Hashooma!
The bandit turns and flees.

Women collapse to their knees and embrace.
Together we are stronger.
She no longer walks there alone.
He will be more devious next time,
         and she more wise.

Closing the Gap

All doubts, however skeptical and cynical they may seem, are really a set of alternate beliefs. ... In fairness you must doubt your doubts.

Timothy Keller

It is the second week in January, and the church has a prayer focus week. Wednesday night a prayer labyrinth is held in combination with the weekly youth night. I think this event is for the whole church. It is, but obviously the majority of patrons know something I don't. Or they just aren't into prayer labyrinths. The idea appeals to me, so I invite a friend to go. About a half dozen other adults brave the generation gap to join the youth. Before entering the darkened sanctuary, the youth pastor briefly instructs us in somber voice: seven stations have been set up and we should take our personal time to move through them. In we go.

At station four I am instructed to contemplate a line from Christ's most famous prayer – *Give us this day our daily bread*. What does *daily bread* mean to us? I stare long and hard at that piece of brown bread in my hand. It does not speak to me, it remains unmoved. The next instruction is to join together with someone else for prayer, *as no one should walk the journey alone*. Well, I don't really want to pray with one of the youth leaders, and now I know why people stayed away ... you have to step out of your comfort zone in a big way. Being the person that is obedient to follow the prescribed format, I sit for a while, and wonder if I can just move on, or should I take a chance and pray with a stranger? Hmm. *Just do it*, comes the inner voice. I try to decide if this is really the Spirit nudging, or my compliance of structure, or my unwillingness. Surely no harm will befall me for connecting with a stranger in prayer, other than being a little uncomfortable.

I finally approach the oldest of the designated prayer partners, a woman of similar age to myself.

"So it says we are to pray with someone."

"Can you give me a little more to go on?" she asks.

I am thinking, *No*, but then say, "You know this segment about contemplating our need for daily bread. I'm not looking for daily bread, I am looking for more than that. Perhaps that should be enough, but truly aren't we called to an abundant life? I am looking for more than simple sustenance."

She seems a bit surprised. After a few more typical words, she speaks of rejoicing in trials and prays that I would have assurance of God's love. With a sigh of relief over a duty done, I move to the next station.

In silent meditation I debate whether the Alka-Seltzer bubbling in the water signifies a release for me. Carol (my now-personal prayer partner) slides in beside me. "Sorry to interrupt, I felt the Spirit nudge me to speak about the assurance of God's love for you, for each of us." She also quotes some appropriate scripture.

"I know all that," I say. "I am struggling to truly believe it." She does not know that I have struggled for almost a decade, coming to terms with God's love for me personally. She looks as though she is searching her mind to find the appropriate comfort verses for me.

"He took two of my children," I speak quietly. "And I have tried to come to terms with how a father shows love by that action. We say action speaks louder than words, and that action spoke volumes." We are both quiet, as she tries to ingest what I have just said. "I know He could have prevented their deaths, I know this action causes the doubts – I would not willingly hurt someone I love by doing that. So, I know in my head all the right things, but my heart struggles."

"You must even feel a little angry at God."

"Not really, funny I never felt angry. I just ... I think I am just disappointed."

"Is your husband supportive?"

Now I don't know how to answer, or should I just laugh? "Well, he has divorced me since ..."

Then my experience and fear of prayer lines and gossip lines crossing rises up. "Please keep this to yourself, I don't share this with many people here."

She assures me of confidentiality. Trying to move on in the conversation, she tries another approach: "So you moved to Cochrane to start a new life? Have you seen the grief program the church is offering?"

"Yes, I was asked if I could lead it." Pause. "But I said no."

"I guess it might be too hard for you," she says.

"No that isn't it. It feels too churchy, I looked at the program, watched part of a video and knew if someone wanted to apply scriptures to all my wounds with a big grin, I would be offended. The church struggles to know how to deal with hurting people." I want to assure her that I'm not feeling hurt by the church anymore, and that I have done a large part of the grief journey already, and that God and I are on good terms; but I feel I've said enough all ready. She can deal with any awkwardness on her own, I don't feel obliged to ease it.

"Perhaps you have been called to go through this, so in time you will be able to offer support to someone else in this scenario." (*Yes, Pat,* I think. Her name is not Pat, but should have been. *Please don't resort to needing a verse-y answer.*) She tells me she will pray for me, and I think she feels the burden of the conversation and her lack of resolution on my behalf.

The next morning, powerful words come to me from a book I divinely chance upon, and I interpret it as a Spirit answer. That book had been hidden for months and that morning I discover several chapters that speak directly to me.

After thirty years as a pastor, R.T. Kendall says,

> The hardest thing in the world to believe is that God really loves us. It is harder to believe that than to believe that there is a God or that Jesus died on the cross or even that He rose from the dead. It's not too difficult to believe that God will take care of you or that "in all things God works for the good of those who love him" though we may not believe that they are for our good at the time ... No, the hardest thing in the world to believe is that God, the true God really loves us right now, just as we are.

My sister-in-law texts while I'm contemplating the above quote. As the phone dings with that familiar sound, I think, *Is that you God?* My sister-in-law and I discuss questions surrounding the assurance of the Creator's love. It has been said that the gap between the head and the heart is the longest eighteen inches, truly a small distance physically, but a large gap emotionally.

I am *becoming* aware that I have my part to play in closing the head-heart gap ... it *becomes* my intention to accept and to believe that God loves me.

In response to my prayer labyrinth evening with her well- intentioned scripted answers, I wrote this poem for Pat and others like her:

Pat Answers

...
   (but did anyone question?)
As much as I like Pat, I do not like her answers.
She conspires with Cliché to resolve my issues.
As though life itself was a problem,
A problem needing a solution
Nailed down with four spiritual laws
and the occasional gut-wrench,
Guidelines, programs and cure boxes to be ticked.

I avoid Pat like the plague.
A cluttery of cutlery
The forked tongue, the butter knife.
With a spoonful of sugar
She speaks up from the benches,
usually has a Word or two to assuage my doubts.
Someone, everyone ... please stop talking, *please*

and just
Be still with me.
Listen for the silence,
for the sound of a breaking heart.
Inhale the pain, the confusion,
Have the courage to
Journey the answerless question with me.

Part Four

Live in each season as it passes; breathe the air, drink the drink, taste the fruit, and resign yourself to the influence of each. Let them be your only diet drink and botanical medicines.

Henry David Thoreau

Seasons of the Soul

Grace grows best in winter.

Samuel Rutherford

Seasonally Affected

> *Autumn is the mellower season, and what we lose in flowers we more than gain in fruits.*
> Samuel Butler

Is it just me, or does fall come more quickly every year? The overachiever boulevard tree turned yellow a week ago, and by now has dropped most of its leaves, disregarding the general population's reluctance to be awed by its splendour. The tree remains unaware that the world is not quite ready for its autumn glory. The back-to-school busses have increased the local traffic; a few tired moms smile with the return of school structure.

Is it possible that one can one get homesick for winter? I didn't think so, but to my surprise I find that while living in Australia, I miss the distinct changes of each season. The near paradise-like daily weather is difficult to complain about. Whenever the Australians complain about their cold temperatures, I mock them letting them know of the minus numbers I had endured in Canada. (*Yes minus 40, yes minus 50 with wind chill.*) My first Aussie winter matches the temperatures of the prairie summer I had left behind. My schoolteacher sister is hesitant to leave her summer, to visit me in Down Under's cold season, only to discover that an Australian winter is more pleasant than a poor Manitoba summer.

Each passing fall makes me realize I'm closer to the autumn of life than the spring or summer. Having grandchildren can be considered another indicator. Instead of begrudging autumn's arrival, lamenting the loss of long summer days, I desire to embrace the season's gifts. Desire alone does not bring results. I enjoy the settled peace of September. Fall brings its own new beginnings. Unlike the artificial new year, where I feel coerced into resolutions of a new direction, fall transitions naturally. The change in weather invites me to try something new, read a book, try a course, dust off my hobbies. Stopping at the Michaels craft store on a cloudy day last week, with forecasts of single digit temperatures for next week, I buy a knitting book! Not any knitting, but arm knitting, where the upper limbs turn into a kind of giant cat's cradle string-game. *You must be going bonkers,* the negative voices in my head chastise me for starting something new, something that I might not complete. My craft room has always been well stocked with unused supplies or projects in need of a final touch. I talk back to those inner critics. "I think it's better to start ten things with enthusiasm, even if I only finish two of them than not to start at all." Much of the enjoyment comes from the exploration of possibilities of the dream, the beginning phases, and the collection of supplies. Does it matter that I might not knit sweaters for my grandchildren like my mother before me? On a positive note, my granddaughter and I try the arm knitting, and she catches on much better than I do.

 I recognize an unidentified longing that perhaps *this next season* will meet expectations, that my desires will be met, that contentment will be achieved; and I realize again that *this is life* and, even more significant, that this is *my life.* I need to live it as it is, where it is, in *this* moment, in *this* season. As much as I wish for it, I cannot go back in time to a previous season ... I do not know what lies ahead, but I have *this* day. I choose to make the most of it. I choose to *become* seasonally adjusted.

Soul Seasons

Every season is one of becoming, but not always one of blooming. Be gracious with your ever-evolving self.
Brittin Oakman

The impact of seasonal change is part of the *becoming* process. There are big seasons in life. There are also seasons of each year, certain things that happen annually like Christmas and your medical. Okay, to be honest my physical does not happen annually. I detest slipping under the sheet for the much younger doctor to inspect my body while reminding me to take calcium and vitamin D. Pretending that neither of us is uncomfortable, the doctor carries on with mundane questions not mentioning the sags, lifting parts up to check underneath. Part of me talks back, letting this doctor (*excuse me, are you old enough to be a doctor?*) know that over two decades ago alien forces started my body make-over, adding dimples or folds in odd places. Part of me is complaining that I had no say in the process. I want a refund on the anti-wrinkle creams I invested in. These physical laments over my aging body can be laughed at, especially in the company of same age females with a glass of wine in (each) hand.

The fact of life is that everyone ages. What is less obvious is that our hearts also respond to the years of emotional toll on them and grief has its own season with fruit that tends to be bitter. However, the soul can grow more beautiful, more *becoming* as it opens itself to the wisdom of each season. In the ancient book of Proverbs, I read, "It's through me, Lady Wisdom that your life deepens, and the years of your life ripen." (Proverbs 9:12).

In our Western culture, Christmas is a major event of the year, with buckets of sadness heaped on those lonely souls already living in the emotional basement. When I venture upstairs beyond the latest Christmas fads and jingles to seek out the deeper seasonal meaning, my spirit is lifted and gifted. The traditional themes of hope, peace, joy, and love are never outdated. One of my favourite quotes of the season is:

> If, as Herod, we fill our lives with things, and again with things; if we consider ourselves so unimportant that we must fill every moment of our lives with action, when will we have the time to make the long, slow journey across the desert as did the Magi? Or sit and watch the stars as did the shepherds? Or brood over the coming of the child as did Mary? For each one of us, there is a desert to travel. A star to discover. And a being within ourselves to bring to life.
>
> Anonymous
> from Sarah Ban Breathnach
> *Simple Abundance*

Each year we choose how we spend our Advent hours. May I take time to feel the desert breeze, to gaze at a star, and to ponder the birth of new understanding. The power of Advent is Immanuel, God with us in each season of life, through the longing and the filling, through the desert and at the oasis.

The Advent-ure Begins with Hope

Hope is the thing with feathers that perches in the soul.
Emily Dickinson

Before the Hallowe'en masks disappear, Christmas merchandise surfaces in the stores. Whenever fresh snow falls before December, the song "It's beginning to look a lot like Christmas," jingles in my head. In 2015, the first snow falls in September when my African grandchildren are visiting. Even though it's time for pyjamas, we dress everyone in the warmest clothes possible to go play outside in the wet snow. That same year also coincides with my first Canadian Christmas without family nearby, so the song loses any glitz well before December. Being solo gives me ample time to explore thoughts behind the season. Discovering the true meaning of the Advent season is my intended focus, with my starting point being to discover if advent and adventure share the same root word. With the ease of Google search, I find out that *advenire*, which means the arrival of something, is at the core of both words.

Advent is defined as the arrival of a notable person, thing, or event, while adventure is an unusual and exciting, typically hazardous, experience or activity. For many children, Christmas is the most exciting time of year, while parents often dread the season. There is an expectancy that fills the air. But, for people in grief, or challenging life circumstances, it is *not* the most wonderful time of the year. And if Santa Claus is the only one coming to town for December 25, I will join the Scrooge crowd with my own Bah Humbug cheer.

In my previous life, I thoroughly enjoyed December festivities, and more recently I've worked intentionally to rekindle a love of the Christmas season. The Christmas of 2005, my worst ever, mocked me with the theme of *all hearts come home for Christmas* – the first Christmas that two of my three children were not on this planet, the first Christmas without my husband. Ten years later I feel a strong kinship with the Biblical descriptor: "The people walking in darkness have seen a great light, on those living in the land of the shadow of death a light has dawned." The darkness is still heavy and the light is only dawning in pale shades, but it is the presence of hope that shines through. The recognition that the great adventure of Immanuel, God with us, through thick and thin, continues.

This solo year in Canada while lighting the first Advent candle of hope, I reflect on the hope that has carried me through a passage of grief, to a new shore. I identify the arrival of hope, in a stumbling towards beauty and grace kind of way. Emily Dickinson compares hope to *the thing with feathers* … does that make hope flighty? Or does it mean hope visits, when I need it most? To perch in my soul, makes me think it might not be permanent, it might not have a good hold. Hope is a choice I can make. For me, the source of hope is the litmus test of its worthiness. Divine hope is at the heart of Christmas. I choose to *become* more hopeful in the advent-ure. Why settle for tinsel, when I am offered hope for eternity?

Peace of Mind Advent-ure

Peace is the result of retraining your mind to process life as it is, rather than as you think it should be.
                                                          Wayne W. Dyer

For peace of mind, resign as general manager of the universe.
                                                          Larry Eisenberg

The slip of the moon shines through the slats of my window blinds, and three segments below that the morning star shines bright and clear. A sense of peace prevails, as I smile back at the moon.

Peace – "a stress-free state of security and calmness that comes when there's no fighting or war" (www. vocabulary. com). Peace – a word passed around like Christmas candy as we light the second Advent candle and wonder how this message of "Peace on Earth, Goodwill to Men" compares against what is going on in the troubling world of the late-night newscast. What replays in our own heads causes even more distress.

While it has been said that time heals all wounds, I think it can also be said that time wounds all heals. Unless I come to terms with what has happened in my life, I cannot stop the whirling activity of the mind. In my past I thought I would be celebrating future Christmases with a large family sitting around my table, three happily married children, and my grandkids adding the extensions so all could nestle around. That plan did not happen the way I had envisioned. And the voices in my head chip away at my fragile peace agreement with life. It now *becomes* my daily choice to stop that loop replay; to accept that my life turned out differently than expected; to declare that there is still much beauty in my life present and to come.

A decade ago, I met a delightful young woman at the drug rehabilitation clinic I worked at in Australia. The clinic founder, Dr. George, asked if I would spend some time with this young woman with a troubled past and an addiction to mass quantities of prescription drugs and alcohol. Over many coffees, conversations, and overdose trips to the emergency department, I got to know her fairly well. Driving in the car one day she told me that there was a constant battle going on for her mind, between an angel on her right shoulder and a little devil on the left.

"I think the left side is winning. I'm always thinking about the next fix. But Jocelyn, you have no idea what it is like to be an addict," she said. She was absolutely right. It is one thing if I'm fighting the desire to finish off the chocolate cheesecake in the fridge, a minor struggle compared to her desperate craving for drugs and alcohol. She is a living example of the struggle Paul writes about in Romans 7: "I can will it, but I can't do it ... I decide to do good, but I don't really do it. I decide not to do bad, but then I do it anyway." She and I discuss these verses many times. My dear friend is not alone in this constant battle of the mind. Peter McWilliams said, "If you want peace, stop fighting. If you want peace of mind, stop fighting with your thoughts."

There is a peace that comes when I get out of my own head to walk in the snow at Christmas time. There is a peace that passes understanding when I seek divine help, and I *become* more peaceful.

The Advent-ure of Joy and SAD
(Seasonal Affective Disorder)

There is nothing so secular that it cannot be sacred, and that is one of the deepest messages of the Incarnation.
                                                    Madeleine L'Engle

After three days of thick fog, fighting for thoughts of Advent- ure joy, I conclude that moving to England or Vancouver will not be in my near future. Three days of not-seeing-across-the-street fog is enough to diminish any joy I've managed to muster up. I need sunshine. The question rises in my mind: *Is my joy up to me?* The answer is not as straight forward as the question implies. After all, I am part of the *Stick a Geranium in Your Hat and Be Happy* generation (Barbara Johnson). While I believe that I have an important part to play, surely I cannot be the sole source of my joy. If so, I am in trouble. And what does joy really mean?

I define joy as a positive state of mind and orientation of the heart, brought about because of the settled assurance that I am not in control of all details of my life. God is alongside, and this brings confidence that ultimately everything is going to be alright. (With thanks to Theopedia and Kay Warren.)

Joy is difficult to find, hard to maintain, and incredibly easy to lose. Richard Rohr says, "*True joy* is harder to hold onto than anger or hatred." I can attest to that; even shallow joy passes that test. To make matters worse, guilt comes along to remind me that I should be more joyful, I should be more grateful. I want to tell him where to go, but initially guilt's familiar voice lures me into a downward joyless spiral. Before long, I'm left to wonder what happened to that joy I was experiencing?

Over time, I have identified some of my joy-thieves, but everyone has their own list. Stress, deadlines, and relationship issues are my major contributing factors. Stress is a rather cliché and open-ended term, but for me it includes having too many choices and technology glitches. I confess that too often technology troubles bring out the worst in my language. Too much hurrying holds hands with deadlines. Hurry often results from my self-imposed deadlines and set start times. While relationships are of utmost importance, maintaining them requires a diligent effort, sometimes more than I have. I feel sad when things go wrong and feelings are hurt. To know what causes the erosion of joy helps me to work proactively to maintain it.

This Advent season I have several little moments of daily joy, and the greatest gift comes through a Christmas drama at the end of this particular foggy week. Had I not invited two friends along, I would have stayed home. It was a night one should have stayed home by the gas fireplace. After a thirty-minute drive in barely-can-see-the-lines fog, our trio arrives in the auditorium, finds our seats and wonders if the fog has followed us inside. Artificially produced haze creates a fuzzy ambiance. Over the next hour and a half, one of the most creative renditions of the Christmas story brings me to tears then laughter and back to tears, as the dancers, actors, narrators, and musicians portray the birth of love and mercy at Christmas. An aerial ring gymnast with Cirque du Soleil precision holds me spellbound for the opening and closing. In a silver bodysuit, the female acrobat takes centre stage to start the production and for the finale, the same dancer, now in red, spins above the stage with sheer beauty and elegance while the chorus sings about Unspeakable Joy. My heart does its own upward spins, nearly lifting me out of my seat. Something within me shifts as the inner fog evaporates and joy invades my spirit. Saturday, the local fog is finally gone, replaced by a dazzling hoarfrost winter wonderland. If you don't know the magic of hoarfrost, imagine everything outside, each branch of each tree, covered with sugar frosting snow diamonds. As I walk, the ancient words of people walking in darkness now seeing a great light comes to mind. When the fog lifts, joy like the hoarfrost covers everything in its path, even the garbage. In the presence of divine beauty, I *become* more joyful.

Love of Advent-ure

To be loved but not known is comforting but superficial. To be known and not loved is our greatest fear. But to be fully known and truly loved is, well, a lot like being loved by God. It is what we need more than anything. It liberates us from pretense, humbles us out of our self-righteousness, and fortifies us for any difficulty life can throw at us.
Timothy Keller

"What does it feel like to be loved?"

That is the question asked of my daughter by her heavily pregnant neighbour. *What does it feel like to be loved?* A haunting question from a woman about to bear her husband a third child. December of 2014, I join my daughter in North Africa to invite neighbourhood ladies to experience the flavours of a Canadian Christmas. In this edge of Sahara country they do not celebrate December 25th, they do not get caught up in ribbons and bows, in getting the right turkey, the right gifts. They do that for other cultural events, but they do not experience the Christmas flurry. As we spread the word about the party, one of the ladies tells me, "Everyone wants to be at your daughter's house." My daughter's house is one of welcome, of light, and love.

In 2015 I cannot be there for the annual Christmas event, but I support my daughter with prayers and encouraging conversations from wintery Canada. She is eight hours ahead, so it's early Friday afternoon when she sends the first party details via WhatsApp: "a house full of women, rich conversation, laughter, fun, food." ... "And one pregnant woman (different from the above one) who does not have the two dinars (about a dollar) for a taxi ride, walked seven kilometres to come." I am moved to tears to read that. That woman walked seven kilometres because she feels love and acceptance from my daughter. My daughter invests herself into the lives of these women – she cares, she listens, she encourages. She also gives this woman a ride home.

What does it feel like to be loved? Years ago, I heard a minister tell a fable by Max Lucado. This is now my retelling of the speaker's tale:

> As the prince rides throughout the land, he takes note of a peasant woman, he falls in love with her ... he proposes marriage. She wants to refuse ... how can he love her? He is royalty and lives in a castle, she is a common woman. He insists that he loves her for who she is, and he insists that he wants to marry her. She still responds in doubt, but as he seems quite persistent, she tells him that she can cook and clean for him and bear his children. He replies,
>
> "I do not want to marry you because you can cook, clean and bear children. I want you to be my wife because I love you." They marry; she cooks, cleans and bears his children, but somehow she never trusts his love. In the end, she leaves him and says to one of her friends,
>
> "I never really felt that he loved me."

My heart stirs at this story because I have often wondered if God, who says He is love, really loves me? What does it feel like to be loved by the Creator of the universe? I have learned that grief does not feel like love and an alcoholic father's mixed messages do not feel like love ... but the question still hangs in the air for me. *What does God's love feel like?* Do God's actions speak louder than His words? How do I resolve the conflict within me of a God who allows suffering? Can I simply choose to believe in a Creator's love? Do I have a part to play in receiving this love? Timothy Keller's above quote assures me that I am not alone in my questions and he challenges me to believe that trusting God's love will fortify me for what will come my way.

As I ponder the greatest gifts of the season, I *become* more hopeful in joy, peace and love. I breathe in the Advent-ure of *becoming*.

The Easter Sting

Easter tells us of something children can't understand, because it addresses things they don't yet have to know: the weariness of life, the pain, the profound loneliness and hovering fear of meaninglessness.
Frederica Mathewes-Green

    That Easter, years ago
    Thoughts that resurrection's promise
    could be the comfort and
    Power to lift the stranglehold of grief.
        Vanity of vanities, all is vanity

    Death, where is thy sting?
    Who dares ask that question?
    That sting
    Is in my heart
    It courses down my cheeks
    It darkens a sunny day
    It knots my stomach tight
    It robs my sleep of dreams by day or night.
    Powerfully absent that victory o'er the grave,
    The grave too fresh, too wrong, two young
        Vanity of vanities

    As time heals all wounds,
    It also wounds all heals.
    It softens grave's sharp edge as
    It mutes bold spring flower

Spring, when do you come
to thaw frozen hearts?
To resurrect life's dreams?
Is it all vanity?

The heavens refuse answer
Victory battles doubts of the mind
Pounds those silent doors
Pleads the prayers of resurrection
Begs for those greater things to be done
Demands that death be overcome as
Sudden hope fuels prayers in the night,
Spirit songs soothe as

Hearts
  Open and the
    Power of the risen Christ
      Envelops our stricken souls

May it be as you have said ...
I believe, help me in my unbelief ...

The Easter Hallelujah

Do not abandon yourselves to despair. We are the Easter people and hallelujah is our song.

Pope John Paul II

I am the song of Easter
Many voices add fullness to my tune
My anthem began before the creation of the world
It took shape and form as earth was birthed
It wandered the wilderness searching a homeland
The aching of the ages
Became visual with the birth of a baby ...
a special child who grew in favour in the eyes of the Lord
a special child who was the Lord.

I am the song of the seasons
The praises formed in the heat of summer
The harvest song of a well lived life
The frozen anguish in the dead of winter,
The irrepressible burst of green life in spring.
I am the song of celebration
The song of beauty

I am the song of despair ... the longing song
How long, oh Lord will you hide your face from us?
I am the song of confusion
Afraid to trust melody with notes unclear
I am the song of plenty, the song of want
The lament of pain, the balm of comfort
I am the song of amnesia,
Words forgotten in the dark of night
I am the song of light and memory
Sing this in remembrance of me

I am the voice in the crowd
Hosanna! Hosanna!
I am the same voice in the crowd
Crucify him! Crucify him!
I am the song of silent shame
And the song of grace and forgiveness
I am the song of strong surrender
The song that hung rugged on the cross ....

I am the song of power ... the resurrection power lives within
I am the song of hope ... green seeded that overflows
Hope to join loved ones again
I am the song of rest, abide in me, sing my lullaby
I am the song within your heart
Come make a joyful noise to the Lord.

We join the song, with voices weak or strong.
This is the song of humanity
The song of a God who sings over us in the night
The song of gratitude, of praise, of sorrow
This is a song unstoppable.

And centuries later I am the receiver of this song
At the graveside of a son, a daughter, a loved one
and I can barely whisper ...
we do not grieve as those who have no hope
Others carry the tune I cannot hold
Spirit sings to aching hearts around the world.

    Will you join the song of a broken Hallelujah?

Pushing through Thick and Thin

How we spend our days is, of course, how we spend our lives. v

Annie Dillard

Daffodil tips poke through dry ground outside my front entrance. Robins have been spotted and the early skies have debuted with fifty shades of sunrise five separate days this past week. As I type, a mourning dove perches on my patio, seeking a quieter spot out of the wind. Yesterday I received a video clip of my grandchildren waving palm branches. All the signs tell me that spring and the Easter season are near.

My mind swirls with ideas for an upcoming talk I'm giving to college-age students. This is the same college my son attended prior to his accident. And I will be speaking on his birthday. Do I mention that? What can I say to them on the given topic of getting through thick and thin that they can relate to? My guess is that the majority of them have not been through major life difficulties yet. At this point they are busy pushing through their studies to get on with real life, a misconception I could dismantle for them. Real life truly is wherever you are, at the moment, it is now. It is not in the future. It is also not in the past. For these students, the words will come from someone considered to have more years in history than in futures.

After being given the topic, I did a search on the meanings and origins of idioms. According to Google, this phrase "through thick and thin" started in the UK in times past when the land was more forested. People cut across the fields to get where they needed to go, and they travelled through *thicket* woods and *thin* woods. I know when I hike in the woods, thickets are places I avoid. Generally in North America, the term means through the good times (thick) and the bad times (thin). I use the comparison of a thick stew or a thin soup, contrasting a hearty stew loaded with nourishing vegetables thickened with meat gravy, perfect on a cold winter's day to a thin soup used for hospital patients after surgery.

My schoolteacher sister uses thick and thin questions for her students in elementary writing. Thick questions prompt a deeper dig into issues, while thin questions address the colour of someone's shirt.

My personal favourite viewpoint arises from the Celtic tradition. Here thick places are when it is hard to get through the chaos of life challenges and events to see God, while the thin places are those times when the veil separating us from God becomes transparent. These thin air spiritual moments allow us to draw closer to God.

What unites both the young college student and the more mature – I can't bring myself to say old – is the challenge to push through all circumstances, thick or thin, to get on to the next. We seem continually dissatisfied with where we are in the present, as if life itself were based on continuous movement. I wish we could all stop pushing through and live the now we've been given.

Childhood offers a reprieve from the tyranny to hustle through, largely because the parents do the hustling. The parental goal is to get the child through teething, sleeping through the night, toilet training, learning to walk, to talk, kindergarten, junior high, high school, university, getting a job and so on and on. The cycle continues as they have children, and begin pushing them through, always living in anticipation or dread of the next thing. All across the prairies we long for spring to push back winter, and for crocuses to push through the ground.

I've experienced two significant times to push. First, women in labour. I've been there both as a nurse and as the mother in labour. In bringing a human to birth, it is not good to push too early: it slows the process. There is a crowning moment to push and push hard. Secondly, in my grief season. Pushing through my doubts and disappointment – not pushing them aside – made it possible to find a foundation to move forward on.

I stop at the local garden nursery this week on a rare, no wind, fifteen-degree, full-of-sunshine day. As the owner packs up my purchase I say, "Isn't it a gorgeous day? Must be good for business. It gets people thinking about gardens early." Without a hint of a smile he responds, "Well as long as we get some good weather when we're supposed to. It doesn't help much now."

I refuse to let him dampen my optimism brought by the sunshine and early warm weather.

Sunday morning the question is asked – Why is so much hype made over Christmas, while the triumph of Easter is played down? Jesus was revolutionary in all aspects: He pushed through death. And that makes all the difference in *becoming* hopeful through the thick and thin.

Part Five

Because Jesus was raised from the dead, we've been given a brand-new life and have everything to live for, including a future in heaven – and the future starts now!

I Peter 1:3-4

Becoming Open: Helps Along the Way

There becomes a new woman
who knows what to do
She has all of eternity
to sift her life through
so while here on earth
      She lets go of things
She laughs and dances in spirited song
She knows ~ she'll *becoming* home soon,
      She doesn't have long ...

Chasing the Light

> *The beauty of imagination helps you ... to venture forth and view the world and your role in it as full of beautiful possibilities. You become aware of new possibilities in how you feel, think and act.*
>
> John O'Donohue

> *Live creatively, friends ... Make a careful exploration of who you are and the work you have been given, and then sink yourself into that. Don't be impressed with yourself, don't compare yourself with others. Each of you must take responsibility for doing the creative best you can with your own life.*
>
> Galatians 6:1 4-5

One fine summer day I shadow my photographer nephew on a job as he chases the light in search of the best image. Time with him energizes me. The morning skies tinged pink, the play of shadows and brightness, angles, shutter speeds, apertures and focus, the golden glow of the lowering sun – a vivid picture for me as we focus on capturing the best light. As Joel pursues the right light to enhance his work, I pursue beauty to energize my imagination and nourish my soul. At the root cause of my reluctance to engage in more artistic ventures is the life-long emphasis put on productivity over creativity.

Growing up in a Mennonite family of six children, the staunchly held belief was that if a man does not work, he shall not eat. This applied as equally to the five daughters as to the last-born son, although the girls thought they had to work much harder than their brother. Out of necessity, productivity was valued over creativity. Creativity and its pursuit happened after the work was done, and in a home with six children, the work seemed endless. But let me tell you, a lot of dancing happened after Saturday chores were done.

At the heart of the matter I succumb too easily to the idea that doing is more important than being. In a Martha world, the Mary endeavours are easily relegated to a time when everything else has been done. Too often I postpone reading a book, dabbling in poetry, craft, or sauntering imaginatively unless I've put in a requisite amount of work. John O'Donohue says that every time you create you are on Holy Ground. Beauty and creativity isn't just about a nice loveliness – it's a more rounded substantial *becoming*, an emerging fullness of grace and elegance.

Compassion and beauty grow within me in direct proportion to the time spent in soul nourishing activities. When I don't take the time they atrophy. This very practical work first model set in earlier life is another default position that needs ongoing adjustment. I laugh as I write this, knowing full well that I'm *wasting* a lot of time playing with words. I've got the wasting it part down – I still need to work on not feeling guilty about it, not needing to justify this time. A favourite descriptor of mine comes from the back cover of *The Shack* by William Paul Young, about living in the wastefulness of grace.

Sunrises, sunsets, moonrises, and moonsets are my favourite ways of chasing the light. One of the most spectacular sunsets I have ever witnessed happened over dinner with two soul sisters. While I lived in Cochrane, two friends arrived annually in February for *The Pink Mountain Retreat*, a time of spiritual growth, conversation, music, shopping, laughter, prayers, and tears. After a beautiful day of rich conversation, riverside walks, and other fun, we sat down to a meal at my dining table. For a full fifty minutes the sunset danced in blazing pinks and orange across the Rocky Mountains in living art form. I don't remember the meal, but I remember our astonishment and delight at the prolonged beauty of the sky. With a glass of wine and fine food we oohed and aahed over the ever-changing light. As I chase the light I *become* lighter in spirit.

The Call of Beauty

Beauty will save the world

          Fyodor Dostoyevsky

In his book *Beauty: The Invisible Embrace*, John O'Donohue expresses the longing, the irresistible urge I feel in the presence of beauty:

> Our deepest self-knowledge unfolds as we are embraced by beauty. In Greek the word for 'the beautiful' is *to kalon*. It is related to the word *kalein* which includes the notion of 'call.' When we experience beauty we feel called ... from aloneness into the warmth and wonder of an eternal embrace.

The question I ponder is, *Why is beauty so important to me?* "When the soul is alive to beauty, we begin to see life in a fresh and vital way." John O'Donohue replies to my query. The answer sounds simple – because it nourishes my soul – but it has a deeper component for me. Beauty calls me (*kalein*) to become part of a grander world than that which surrounds my sometimes small life.

Simone Weil has said, "Only two things pierce the soul. One is pain; the other beauty." In the aftermath of tragedy, or in a phase of life where disappointments stack higher than the shrinking good, beauty tips the scale in favour of hope. Sometimes life overwhelms and a person needs to pause. Beauty is my reset button. Sitting in the presence of beauty provides that needed pause. Beauty allows my soul to breathe again, restores my courage, reminds me that the sun will rise again the next day and that life is truly worth living.

In an artsy boutique store in St Petersburg, Florida, I first see the words of William Morris: "Have nothing in your house that you do not know to be useful or believe to be beautiful." I adopt this mantra as my own. I may not always practice it, but it simplifies my shopping. My oldest sister's words also come to mind: *You don't have to own something in order to appreciate its beauty.* At times I feel this strong need to purchase a beautiful item, striving to have an item help fill the deep void of intangible loss. The greatest beauties, those of nature and of good relationships, cannot be purchased to display in my house. Often I happily err on the soul side of purchases.

For decades I've been a flower champion, choosing to plant more daisies than tomatoes. It did not take me long to realize that I can buy better veggies at the markets than my blighted tomatoes and my accidental mini carrots. But the flowers, they sense my appreciation, they come through for me, bringing smiles, creating bouquets of cheeriness, and deep inhales of contentment and fragrance. Their names speak of poetry, like "subtle sacraments of colour" (John O'Donohue). There are few poems to the lowly but functional tomato, potato or green bean. Beauty speaks of love. Wisteria in bloom engages me with a mystical essence of beauty. To witness tiny blossoms in unexpected and remote places; by that evidence alone, I *become* aware that the Creator of life loves beauty. And I am freed to love beauty and to *become* more beautiful in spirit as well.

Kayak Moon Chasing

> *To behold beauty dignifies your life; it heals you and calls you out beyond the smallness of your own self-limitation to experience new horizons. To experience beauty is to have your life enlarged.*
>
> John O'Donohue

Seize the moment, make the most of everyday experiences, add the artistic flair to life.

That moment, that one fall morning, I become moon chaser extraordinaire as I follow the setting of the full moon. My kayak is loaded the day before in the hope of catching the full moon setting over the water with the Rocky Mountains as a backdrop. From my West window an hour before set time, I see the round orb, and I can see that low clouds are a potential moon cover-up risk. But I pack up tea, muffin, banana, nuts, notebooks, cameras – mighty are the preparations. Don't forget mittens, socks – it's bound to be cold on the water.

Ghost Lake, fifteen minutes to the west, is my intended destination; however, as I near I can see that the hills surrounding the lake obstruct the moon's descending pathway. As I reach the turnoff to the lake, I wonder if I should keep following the moon, or stick to the original plan to kayak here anyway. For a brief second I hesitate, but my Rav4 decides to stay in pursuit, and it turns off about five miles further up the road at what looks like the right direction for a moon view. The road twists and turns as more daylight arrives. While I know it's a not a race against the clock, it will still be a challenge to find the right location to watch the moon gracefully sink below the Rockies.

I have a brief conversation with Mother Nature: "Don't you want to grace me this day, as I did get up early to see this? I made the effort, don't you want me to watch in wonder?" In her gentle way, she doesn't let me know how presumptive my question is. I remember the missed photograph of over a year ago, where the full moon set in fashionable glory against the pink Rockies. That day I was given the sighting, the perfect picture, but I lacked the time as I was meeting friends and I hadn't factored in extra photography time. This day I can stop, but the moon isn't compliant to my wishes.

As I round one bend in the road, several longhorn cattle are at rest in the pasture, up close and personal. I stop and get out of my vehicle, trusting the skinny barbed wire fence to keep the massive animals and I separated. The mist curls from the steer's nostrils, backlit by the sun. Click, click, click. Snapping several shots, I move closer to catch the one whose face is turned in my direction. In the background I see a different beast start to paw at the ground. I wonder about the strength of the fence as the near one decides to rise to greet me. Quickly I snap a few more and carry on with my travels. No need to put any fence or pawing bulls to the test.

Onwards I go, knowing that the moon has set. The next decision I face: do I go back to Ghost Lake or proceed another twenty-five minutes towards the mountains? Voices of reason battle the desire to just do it, but I ignore them; chastising myself again for being irresponsible. What will my epitaph read? She studiously attended to all her duties? Or she was a seeker of beauty, and sometimes it got in the way of duties? Today, my duty is to heed the call of beauty.

The mountains win. I turn right, heading west. Golden trees beckon me further. By now I know I am headed to Gap Lake. Highlight of fall beauty, this small lake couldn't be more stunning, the snow-capped mountains reflected in the mirror-calm water as I arrive. While driving, I scan the rocks and ledges for the Rocky Mountain sheep that frequent this area. When they appear I always view them as a gift. No sightings this day. I turn off the highway onto the trail to the lake and as I spin my vehicle around to offload my kayak, they appear. Hidden above the ridge, but in plain sight of the lake, the sheep stare back at me, my mouth wide open, their mouths munching.

A big thank you smiles across my face. Offload and slip into the water ... the tea is still warm, the air cool and only my left sock gets slightly damp as I near dry dock into my kayak. The rest is magical history. A picture may paint a thousand words, but I only have words to respond to the beauty, words of praise which spontaneously erupt from within – songs to the open fresh mountain air. I wanted another chance to kayak a mountain lake, and it happened because I have become responsive to the call of beauty over doing. Thank you, Lord!

Conversations with I AM

God said to Moses, "I AM who I AM. This is what you are to say to the Israelites: 'I AM has sent me to you.'"
Exodus 3:14, NIV

You walk on water, You walk with me, You hold my right hand.
The longing, the aching I felt on Mother's Day as we sang

Better is one day in your courts than thousands elsewhere.
My children have had ten years of one day in your court
And I have had thousands elsewhere …
And yet, the longing the aching to be with you, with them

Help me Jesus . . .   I AM

You answer with I AM?
When I say, Help me,
>*You say, I AM*
When I say, Walk beside me,
>*You say, I AM.*
When I say, Live in me,
>*You say, I AM*
When I say, Are You listening?
>*You say, I AM*
Your name says it all, Is that what you are trying to tell me?
>*I AM*
Thank You, Jesus, that brings me a smile.
>*Me too.*

And I can already hear the doubts,
the unbelief question of this conversation,

and I say, *Help thou my unbelief,* and
>You say, *I AM.*
And I say *Thank You* and you kindly say
>*You're welcome.*

Part Six

She understands now what she, in all her worry, had forgotten. That even as she hesitates and wavers, even as she thinks too much and moves too cautiously, she doesn't always have to get it right. It's okay to look back, even as you move forward.

Jennifer E. Smith
The Comeback Season

Stumbling Towards Grace and Resolution

Footwear for the Journey ...

Shoes for the curator of my soul
Cement blocks, ill-fitting shoes
    Doubt on the left
    Fear on the right
    Laced with guilt
It is hard to walk
    Harder to dance
        Impossible to fly
            Barefoot she skips ahead.

Victory Redefined

> *I've looked at life from both sides now,*
> *from win and lose and still somehow,*
> *It's life's illusions I recall.*
> *I really don't know life at all.*
>
> Joni Mitchell

I've participated in a faith-based writing group that asks us to respond to a monthly blog question. One month the question is: *How did you find your way to victory?* This query almost throws me for an existential crisis loop. This is my somewhat revised response to that question . . .

She comes to a point in life where she realizes that the victory story is the most acceptable and expected in church circles. Everyone in the wooden pews rejoices to hear the testimony of she-who-has-overcome, and she who-is-back among the blessed. Kleenexes fly from purses to dab at the corner of sincere eyes as the story of her overcoming is repeated. Cowering in the back is another she. The *she* who still hopes for victory, the *she* still in need of a miracle. The *she* who still feels defeated. They are waiting until she enters the victory ring in order to welcome her back into the defined fold ... she also waits and senses the ever-widening gap. Where can she go? After all the prayers spoken and the initial promising signs of a win, the fatal cancer reappears, the marriage crumbles, the prodigal son remains aloof, the alcohol wins, the money is gone ... no apparent victory in sight. The scriptures taunt her with hope not realized. What good is hope with its false expectations and vague consolation? She finds it safer to live in the flatline of despair because she is welcome there. She doesn't have to fake victory, in fact it would be disruptive. *Hello darkness, my old friend, I've come to talk to you again.**

Yet something new stirs in her soul. It takes time ... but, she realizes that she is still breathing, she is still talking to God, and she feels the touch of beauty again. She has endured what she would have deemed unendurable earlier, she never thought it possible for people to live through what she has just lived through ... she begins to believe that survival is underrated and that victory has more than one representation. Perhaps victory is not the lofty goal, just perhaps she is still blessed. For now she keeps these thoughts to herself.

I have been that *she* ...

Years before the *she* episode, I attended a church committee meeting. Someone in the group suggested that we should not share stories of excessive hope, because it could leave us feeling discouraged.

"Let's face it," he said, "the average person holding down a pew isn't going to experience the same miracle that our last speaker did. Aren't we dangling false hope in front of our members?"

While I understood both sides of that equation, I was taken aback at the question. Perhaps it was his honesty. But if all we heard was doom and gloom stories (and there were plenty), added to a long list of thou shalts and shalt nots, wasn't there a danger of suffocation by grey legalism? Why did we accept that it was easier to live with a sense of resignation than to risk hope because it might be dashed?

Victory implies winning over a situation. Perhaps it is time to redefine the concept of victory. Truly, to survive loss and then to rejoin the journey of daily life with a smile on the face is a giant victory step. Victory is learning to live with hope again; victory is trusting the giver of that hope even when it may seem irrational. In that sense, I am *becoming* victorious.

(*Thank you, Paul Simon, for that well-known line.)

My Choice

Hope is a choice
Hope has given me my voice
to question to doubt, to scream, to shout.
Hope has been in the midst
as a spark
as a river
a cause to shiver.
Hope behind, hope before
Hope surrounds as it opens
and shuts the door.
The taste of hope
And I want more.
More of the source
more of the truth
more of the grace it has given.
I want Hope on this earth
And a taste of Heaven.

Moniker Matters ... What's in a name?

Look, I've written your names on the back of my hands.
Isaiah 49:16

Being the fifth child, the fifth girl, I'm surprised my mother still had a few creative names left over. All four of my older sisters had two names, and my mother thought outside the customary name box of her Mennonite era. My mother was a fan of the Lennon Sisters and thought that five girls was great; my father wished I was a boy. I believe I owe my life to my brother. Had he arrived ahead of me instead of sixteen months later, I might not have been conceived. I've thanked him many times for being younger than me.

When I came along as girl number five, my guess is that my mother used whatever names she had left in her wish bag, Jocelyn and Bonnie, with Marie added for a half sister-in-law. As an adult I asked my mother: "Did you really name me after Tante Marie?" She paused before answering, "I guess so, but I don't know why I would have." My mother chuckled as she told me this. I think there was a sense of gratitude to Tante Marie. In her desire to do good, she looked after the gaggle of girls my mother dropped off at her place. But, if we were dressed in pants, we returned home wearing cousin Martha's skirts, a one size that did not fit all, but adorned us nonetheless. Tante Marie believed girls should wear skirts. Tante Marie comes to mind as the critic voice for my writing, the one who wants me to write in a skirt, whether it fits or not, because that would be the dress code for good girls to write in.

Whether or not my Tante was a factor in my third name, Marie carries the meaning of a wished-for child, besides meaning both rebellious and bitter. Jocelyn is a name that means joyful, and my mother strung the names together as Jocelyn Bonnie Marie. When I was born, the aunts and uncles on my mother's side (Tante Marie being on the other side) called me by my second name, Bonnie. Once school started, because there was another Bonnie in the class whose first name was Bonnie, the teacher decided that I should be called Jocelyn, as that was my legal first name. It surprises me that the teacher carried the power to change someone's name at the time, but I am grateful to her for giving me back my name. When I was married at age twenty-one, I had uncles tell me that they still thought of me as Bonnie; and I always replied with a joyful Jocelyn smile.

While I lost the Bonnie by kindergarten, with my return from Australia I feel the need to lose another name. What to do with my surname now that the marriage was done? The person returning from Australia is a person in transition, she is becoming someone new. In response to dramatic life events we are participants in the choice to grow or wither. We participate to become something better. My spirit and skin tone had blossomed under the Aussie sun.

What's in a name? Ask an expectant mother who spends hours pondering names. Ask the paint and plant people. I have purchased both paints and plants because of their names. I chose Banana Cream Pie over stark white, I would have opted for Coconut Cream had they offered it. The summer after the accident, a plant named Brittanica grew tall in the rock garden that my daughter Brittany helped design four years earlier. The summer my marriage eroded, Love Lies Bleeding with its magenta red tassel flowers flourished in proximity to the Bleeding Hearts. An abundance of floral bleeding mirrored my life that summer. So what's in a name? It speaks both of who we are and what others wish for us.

The majority of names and labels are bestowed upon us. With my divorce finalized, I wondered – what to do about my surname? I married at the start of an era when women had options to keep their own names; there was also a lot of hyphenation happening. Personally, I had been firm on the side to take my husband's surname, in fact I debated strongly with my friends that it indicated commitment. At the same time, The Mennonite Treasury, the recipe book all Mennonite girls received as a shower gift, included recipes submitted by the generations previous, authored by the likes of a Mrs. Peter Kroeker, a Mrs. George Friesen, a Mrs. Isaac Hildebrand. Interesting that this caught my attention, as I knew for a fact that it wasn't Peter, George or Isaac cooking. You are not Mrs. Isaac, are you? In the seventies most of my friends adopted their husband's surnames as well. It is fascinating to observe the changes in cultural norms in our identity, roles, and titles and to observe my generation's progression of ideas as we age.

My mind focuses on my name issue as I return from Australia to live in Canada. A year earlier, my sister-in-law had recommended that I register for a speaker's conference in Grand Rapids, Michigan. The registrar is delighted with an Australian attendee. I disappoint them in not having an

Aussie accent, although I have opportunity to use G'day, mate and No worries. One of the conference sessions is on acronyms and catchy titles. The idea of my name change whirls in my mind without a place to land. I want my name to indicate the new status, not as a divorcee, but the signification of a new person. "What, you just make up your own name?" my inner critic voice asks in disdain. Reverting back to my maiden name does not feel like a suitable option. I have not been Krahn for decades, but if I go with Krahn there is no legal fee for a name change. Something else will cost money and will be a little more complicated.

In that acronyms workshop, and after a lot of prior conversation with God, I play with the alphabet. Letters and meanings swirl and land on the page … and I am given a new name:

F-A-I-R-E

Faire – pronunciation the same as my surname of the last 30 years. Thus I can still maintain my name connection as the mother of my two children, Jordan and Brittany Fehr, but this is different. The beauty of my name catches in my throat, sending shivers up my spine as the words come to me, in my time of identity crisis, divorce crisis, and God where-are-you-in-this-move-back-from-Australia crisis, this what-am-I-to-do-now, where-will-I-go crisis saddled with an old identity that no longer fits. The name descends gently. FAIRE – the name given by the Spirit to signify Faith And Identity Restored Eternally. A holy moment of divine affirmation. I pause in wonder, smile, and then I'm eager to share my new name with my sisters.

God comes through with brilliance. I feel I'm standing alongside Sarai/Sarah with her name change, beside Abram/Abraham, Jacob/Israel, and the Apostle Saul/Paul. God has been in the renaming business for a while and I sense the personal touch. In that acronyms workshop He reminds me that I am called out by name and that I am loved. God and I have a private chuckle when I realize that we just got the H out of Fehr.

My new name is becoming me.

Home is Where you Hang your Heart ...

Home is not just the place where you happen to be born. It's the place where you become yourself.

Pico Iyer

In the process of becoming, I am far removed from what I call my previous life. That was another planet, an episode of *The Blessed Western Life* sitcom with three children, one husband, prescribed faith system, four-bedroom home, and a cat that ran away. The heart-warming family drama was a part of the before life. Everyone must have a before life, before they were where they are now; and in the midst of now, the before can hold incredible nostalgic appeal. Yet life happens for all, rarely as first planned. Children grow up, jobs change, people die, relationships end. Suddenly Plan B crashes into effect without our consent. People continue to be surprised and devastated that life does not go as planned or as expected or as hoped for.

After the Australian sun infuses new life into my soul, I quickly discover that I do not have the financial resources required to stay in the land down under without a job. Too young to retire but determined that I will not work full time as a nurse in a private hospital, I ponder my options. Where to go, what to do? After serious consideration on various fronts, the words in Jeremiah 31:23 take on new meaning: "Set up signposts to mark your trip home. Get a good map. Study the road conditions. The road out is the road back." In convoluted fashion, this becomes my clarifying verse and inspiration for a return to Canada. Twenty-seven months earlier I'd left for Australia, hoping to find myself or forge a new self and now the time has come for that woman to discover the road back. The return to Canada was not to be confused in my mind as a failure, but to be seen as a change of venue for further growth.

Physical landscapes are easier to modify than the minefields of the mind. Many people find it easier to plod on in a difficult known than to move into the unknown. And yet radical life changes require radical responses from me. As supportive as my former hometown had been for raising a family, I know that I am not ready to return there. I may be homeless but I am not helpless. What next? turns into What next, Papa? (Romans 8:15).

This becomes another adventure, somewhat challenging, but not overwhelming. Briefly I wonder if *unanchored* can be considered an address. While I want to experience life in other locations, I know that Australia will be extremely difficult to match. The idea of Western Canada, possibly Calgary, takes root. It has a vibrancy that might rival Perth's multiculturalism, pedestrian friendly downtown, and bike trails. The nearby ocean and endless blue skies of Perth can be exchanged for the majestic Rocky Mountains. There is that little factor called winter – no getting around that one in Canada – but I am also certain that the cockroach count will be down. With contemplation and prayer, I start the online search for places to rent in Calgary. One night I have a dream – more like a vision, a divine vision – and in it I see a large green road sign that says *Cochrane 13 km*. This is very curious. In the morning I call my daughter and ask her, "Kristen, what do you think about Cochrane?"

"Oh mom, it's beautiful, I was just there. Do you remember Kaylee my roommate from Columbia College? Well, she's married and they live in Cochrane, it's a great place."

For many of the earlier years in my previous life, we went family skiing in Banff, Alberta. We traveled down the Trans-Canada Highway, and passed the sign that pointed to Cochrane. On one of those trips I said, "It would be nice to see Cochrane one day."

I first see it on a day in mid-July 2011. An Australian friend is visiting Canada and we drive to the Rocky Mountains via Cochrane. There I see the same signpost I saw in my dream: *Cochrane 13 km.*

My heart beats a little faster as we travel north along Highway 22. When my eyes encounter the Bow River carving its blue ribbon through the green forest valley, my immediate thought is, *I could live here.* I had not arranged any viewing appointments, but Nicky and I stop at a realtor who refers us to another realtor who deals with rental properties and we meet Eleanor K.

"I think I have one place," she says. "It just came up yesterday. It's available September 1st."

"Can we see it?"

"Not today. I have to give twenty-four hours' notice to the current occupants." We arrange to view the condominium on our return trip. Forty-five minutes to the west we spend three days in the beauty of the mountains of Banff National Park and return at the appointed time on Saturday. I am giddy with delight as we walk into the unit.

The west facing window draws me in. I hold my breath as I move forward. What to my wondering eyes should appear but the Rocky Mountains – they should have come with eight tiny reindeer. It feels like Christmas. *I could live here*, I think for the second time.

"I'll take it," I say to Eleanor. We discuss rent, references, and a few other items. The first of September, I move into my dream place. This prairie girl with her prairie bicycle legs has a place in the shadow of the Rocky Mountains, a scenery change of significant elevation.

After a year of renting and contemplating if this is where I want to make my home, my condo unit comes up for sale. Should I stay, should I purchase, should I find a different place? Cochrane is the place I want to remain, and after viewing several other places, this condo remains my first choice. This is my first time ever to put in an offer to purchase a property. Formerly it had been my husband who made or initiated the big financial decisions. It is both daunting and exhilarating to decide this on my own. It is one thing to make an offer to purchase; I did not realize the hurdles a single woman has. Lorrie, the financial broker guides me through the loan process. The paperwork, the multiple forms asking the same questions, requiring repeated confirmation that I can finance the mortgage. Dreams do need backing, I understand that. What I do not understand is when Lorrie calls to say, "I need a copy of your divorce certificate."

"You need what?! Why?" She tells me the "divorce" status impacts my rating. Had I been "single" it would be better.

"Try to get your accountant to change the status," she advises.

Seething, I produce divorce certificates. *What does that have to do with anything? My tax forms indicate I can carry the mortgage. I bet men don't have to produce them.* But I bite my tongue, mostly – Lorrie hears my complaints. After all the back and forth to get the right papers, etc., my Stamp of Approval arrives before the bank receives the final paperwork with my divorce certificate. Go figure!

During that loan application process, background issues associated with approval surface. The religious notion to "study to show thyself approved" has weighed me down for years in trying to earn approval. As a child, a report card 'A' brought approval. In my mind performance correlates with both my earthly father and my heavenly father's acceptance and love. Now the loan process raises the divorce status issue, which had also met with great disapproval in many of my previous circles. That approval default is being kindly reset at this point in my life as I search for a new home to hang my heart.

Louise Hay says, "You've been criticizing yourself for years, and it hasn't worked. Try approving yourself and see what happens." I am *becoming* more at home with approving myself and less concerned with others' disapproval.

Ride the Moving Wave

It's never too late – in fiction or life – to revise.
                                        Nancy Thayer

Moving, in and of itself, has never been a holy event in my life. Some of my least holy language spills out under the last day packing pressure. The advice columns tell me to be decisive when handling items. Handle every article only once, decide: do you take it, donate it, or junk it?

If only it was that easy. How had I collected so many bits and pieces of paraphernalia in my time living in this mountain paradise? An oversized van and my mother's small car, both with tires bulging, transported all the carefully selected items across three provinces to begin my new life in Alberta. A bed, a chair, a lamp, pictures, papers, some books, and too much clothing buoyed my anticipated new beginning. Not one face was familiar to me on my arrival, and half a decade later both the stuff and my relationships have mushroomed exponentially into the beautiful life developed in this region. Daily the mountains' grandeur reshaped my soul to look upwards, to take deep gulps of clear fresh air, and to take the needed time to process life.

What the experts don't tell me is how to pack up the benefits reaped while living here. How do I box up the richness of relationships to take to the next location? And in the relocation process, I ponder what it means to be at home. My soul has found a resting place, a nesting place here.

When people would ask what brought me to Cochrane, I would say it was a series of events. My tragic history was tightly held from the casual questioner. Most people didn't know how to respond if I would say, "I lost two children in a car accident and my marriage fell apart. I couldn't stay, I needed to go."

And now a rapid series of events fuelled by Cupid's arrow draws me back to my prairie home province. Can I allow myself to live in this new land of dreams? It feels scary to even contemplate. While there has been a longing in my heart and soul to move on, at times it feels more comfortable to remain in the quiet identity I've built, the identity of a grief survivor. It seems unthinkable that I can experience deep joy in a partnered relationship again. And yet, I am smitten. I've been given the gift of a fantastic partnership of a lifetime and I am riding the wave. Many friends clap their hands with this turn of events. They tell me that I deserve this ... and I wonder if I do deserve to be so happy? That question begs the other question: did I deserve the tragedy?

In the movie, *The Second Best Exotic Marigold Hotel*, Maggie Smith's character asks, "Is identity like clothing? How often can you redefine yourself?" With obvious disdain, Judy Dench as Evelyn Greenslade replies, "As often as we choose to."

A wall hanging jammed into a box says, *In the end, what matters most is how well did you live, how well did you love, how well did you learn to let go?* As I pack, I let go of stuff. I pack up fond memories, rich friendships and lessons learned. I can move to this next phase of life a much richer person having spent five years near the Rockies. I am confident that the mountains will continue to unfold, even from the Prairies.

Rebuilding Walls

The walls you're rebuilding are never out of my sight.
Isaiah 49:16

"Perhaps this will be the year" are the final words of my daughter's home-sending prayer following my visit to her family in North Africa, March 2016. Inwardly I roll my eyes: *Nice to have some optimism, Kristen, but this is not the first time we've prayed for a possible life partner.* She and I lie side by side on the guest bed, eyes heavenwards, hearts united. This has been an ongoing desire, but along with that desire comes the increasing acceptance that perhaps I will live the rest of my life solo. In fact, I have become comfortable with the idea that I might be better off solo.

Let me backtrack a bit. Mentally, coming to this conclusion involves numerous laughable events along the way and some amusing dating experiences. How does a woman in her late fifties meet someone? Initially, I thought it might happen within the church setting or dance classes, or with a volunteer position. I soon realize that church is geared for couples and families with young children; women outnumber men five to one at dance lessons and in the volunteer positions I hold. After some initial reluctance, I follow a niece's advice for online dating. She says, "We do almost everything online, so why not meet someone on a dating site?" It worked well for her. Nothing ventured nothing gained; I'll give it a try. Besides that, I won't let anyone know that I am online.

First, let me tell you that online dating is not for the faint of heart, but it proves interesting.

Second, it is not like the movies where the beautiful looks-like-her-picture female always finds the equally perfect looks-like-his-picture male. In my age category, attractive women outnumber handsome men, but most men still think they are forty, looking for someone ten years their junior. More importantly, how can I judge good character in a space where people say anything they want, true or imagined? What I have to work with is a few mostly doctored pictures or some that should have been. Sorry guys, those selfies taken from the stomach angle double both your gut and your nostril size; selfies from the bathroom mirror don't need the flash, as it obliterates half your face! And please use spell check – especially if you want me to know you are *carning lovening all wase smileing.and very quide.* (I think he meant to say *caring, loving, always smiling, and very quiet.*) Early in this venture I seriously contemplate a new work-from-home business of helping men write winning profiles.

    Following fill-in-the-blank prompts, I have to decide what am I looking for in a man. *Hmm, is Richard Gere on this site?* The prompts don't ask the right questions. Although there is space to add your personal free-flow ideas, most men leave this section blank. Some of the questions help me narrow the parameters: definitely a non-smoker, definitely near enough to meet. Well, the first person I do agree to meet is at least 700 miles away.

    Seven hundred miles fails the distance criteria, but after some online conversations, he claims business in the area and arranges a meeting. He checks off as a non-smoker. After our meeting, I wonder about his persistent cough. Did he have a cold? Finally, during our next phone call the nurse in me asks, "So how long have you not smoked?" A rather nervous cough, followed by his confession: "six weeks." Exactly three days after he'd read my profile, so he could claim nonsmoking status. *Well,* I think, *at least he is trying.*

I give him the benefit of the doubt, but it is the double scoop that does him in. Even though he is a diet-controlled diabetic, he has a double scoop of ice-cream. I know many of us, myself included, might have a double scoop, but not after he asks my opinion on sugar content single versus double, and then goes ahead in spite of my medical suggestion. Why bother to ask me? I remember an aunt who married later in life to a man with diabetes and I am not here to nurse someone with diabetic complications. Still takes me too long to write the Dear John letter.

After a few more awkward episodes of Christian Mingle, it is time to take to heart the words that have encouraged me since my divorce: "And don't be wishing you were someplace else or with someone else. Where you are right now is God's place for you. Live and obey and love and believe right there. *God, not your marital status, defines your life.*" (1 Corinthians 7:16, emphasis mine).

Too long I've allowed my (post)marital status to define my life negatively. This view is reinforced with my weekly phone calls to my mother. Two genres of questions frequent our conversations.

Mother: "So are you working?"
"Yes mom, I'm doing some volunteer work and some writing."

"But are you doing something that you get paid for?"

"No, I'm living off the proceeds of crime." My personal joke that she misses. (In some churchy circles being divorced is akin to a crime.)

Next she asks, "Have you met anyone?"

"No."

"Well, what's wrong with you?" (*Thanks, Mom. It's not as though I'm not wondering the same thing.*)

After a while, I tune out with these questions, realizing that her increasing dementia is removing her social filters. Ordinarily, she would not be that direct or critical of me.

One Sunday I call, she asks the usual dating questions, and I tell her, "I have gone out a few times Mom, but honestly I haven't met anyone that meets my standards."

A short pause, then she says, "Well, maybe you should lower your standards."

Another short pause. Simultaneously we burst into the belly laughter that brings tears to our eyes.

"Sorry, that is not good advice," she admits.

"No, Mom," I agree, "that's not good advice, and I don't plan to follow it."

Spring of that year, I feel that I am done with the search for someone to complete me. It is time to acknowledge, celebrate, and own my singleness. My middle sister and I make exciting plans for a South American trip. A month later with two dear friends in Clear Lake, Manitoba, I announce,

"You know, I think I'm going to be single for the rest of my life, and I'm going to be ok with that. This is my declaration."

These two precious women know my heart, have journeyed with me through much of the thick and thin of grief, divorce, living in the loss, and through the looking-for-beauty-when-life-throws-you-ugly moments. These ladies regularly mop up the cries of my heart, and here over the kitchen island I declare my coming to terms and embracing my singleness. Victory!

Two days later, a friend and former colleague asks if we can have lunch. We had spent some time together over the winter, but he'd met someone. *Now he wants dating advice,* I think, and I do not feel inclined to advise him on how to pursue the other woman. (*Some men can be so obtuse! He could have been an interest.*) But I am heading back to Alberta in a few days, so what do I have to lose? I can advise him and then get back to my newly declared single life.

It turns out that he doesn't want dating advice, other than to let me know that he is available to date. (*Now I am the obtuse one thrown into a tailspin.*) The next day, instead of driving back to Alberta, my Rav4 and I fly across three prairie provinces wondering what just happened. That lunch sets off a whirlwind of FaceTime calls and messages over the summer. He plans to visit for five days at the end of August. My anxiety level goes up when he adjusts his work schedule to extend our time together. *What if this does not go well? What will I do with him for that long?* By the time he arrives, I feel fairly confident that it will go well.

It goes well enough that he proposes the day he arrives. We take a few days to process our decision before we let our children know. When I introduce Harold to my mother, with a twinkle in my eye, I assure her that I did not lower my standards.

Four months later we marry using the words from Isaiah as our theme:

> The walls you're rebuilding are never out of my sight. Your builders are faster than your wreckers. The demolition crews are gone for good. Look up, look around, look well! ... As sure as I'm the living God – God's decree – you're going to put them on like so much jewelry, you're going to use them to dress up like a bride. (Isaiah 49:16-18)

How reassuring to me that this journey of *becoming* has been and continues to be under divine supervision.

Let me Bloom

If I am to bloom
Let me be persistent as the dandelion,
rare as the orchid,
beautiful as the iris,
hopeful as the tulip,
sunny and climbing as bougainvillea.
Let me be the first crocus of spring,
the last mum in the fall snowflakes.
Oh let beauty burst forth in flower,
Let my petals drip goodness and passion.
You have called me to bloom.
Inhabit my days with your
Grace and Beauty.

And when the blossom is spent
May I mature into the best damn foliage around.

    At some point she decides that the accident is not going to be the closing mark on her life. She wants to create another ending – something like she lives happily ever after.

Epilogue

The only person you are destined to become is the person you decide to be.

Ralph Waldo Emerson

For nearly a decade, ideas of *becoming* have rattled around in my brain. It is time to release these rattlings before I turn into a crotchety old woman. A number of things transpire to urge the process. For one, I turned sixty-five and I realize that the years have a tendency to slide by. While my hindsight has grown in clarity ... or is it just my behind sight that grows? Either way it is time to release the words.

Secondly, the COVID-19 pandemic unfolds all around me. For all the disaster meetings I attended over the years as a nurse, I'm thankful it remained a hypothetical event in my career. End times or not (I think it speculative to place the Apocalyptic end into this pandemic) we all have a time to face our own thoughts of winding down rather than gearing up. Not only did I turn sixty-five, but within COVID definitions that suddenly categorized me as *elderly*. My days rapidly number after that, adding a sense of urgency to finish this book.

And, alongside the pandemic, Black Lives Matter has become a powerful movement. Amen to that – the time is ripe. Reflecting on that, it is important to realize that all lives matter, and that people's stories matter. This is an interesting time to be alive.

For fifteen Februarys, I've carried a customary ache in the pit of my stomach. For fifteen years I've tried to hold on to the warmth of the last time I hugged my son and my daughter. The deep sadness still catches me off guard. I'm not surprised at the lingering pain, instead I marvel at how life twists and turns to re-inflict loss. In Hosea 11, I come face to face with a God also longing for his child: "When Israel was only a child, I loved him ... I lifted him, like a baby, to my cheek ... how can I give up on you Ephraim? How can I turn you loose, Israel?" And my journal entry of that February morning reads: *God you miss us when we are separated. You understand my grieving. And you love me. I am beginning to believe it. Why? Because your spirit hovers near like a parent. A parent who wants the child to become. And I say Thank you, You've been here all along.*

When I think about the universality of suffering, I'm amazed at the number of walking wounded ever among us. I'm also amazed at the power of hope and the resiliency of the human spirit. After a serious attack of malaria my oldest daughter said:

"I do not want to go through this much pain, without learning everything I can from it."

Sometimes I tire of the hard learning and feel overwhelmed with the prevalence of loss. Other times I marvel at the joy of discovery made on this journey of *becoming*. I recognize that it remains my choice to seek the gifts that come with the pain, my choice to *become* at peace with the mystery of suffering. I'm learning that God's nearness provides a soothing for the soul. I'm learning that speaking myself in the direction I want to go is what I must do. I'm learning that life is this never ending, always changing journey. I'm learning that trust moves me forward to *becoming*. I'm aware that I live in a world that still holds much beauty.

And I'm learning what it feels like to be loved.

It is *Becoming* Me ...

Recommended Books

Sarah Ban Breathnach, *Simple Abundance*
David Benner, *The Gift of Being Yourself: The Sacred Call to Self-Discovery*
Ruth Harms Calkin, *The One Year Book of Bible Promises*
Julia Cameron, *Transitions*
Jeanine Cummins, *American Dirt*
Peter Enns, *The Bible Tells Me So*
Peter Enns, *The Sin of Certainty*
John and Stasi Eldredge, *Captivating*
Dali Lama and Desmond Tutu, *The Book of Joy*
Anne Lamott, *Small Victories*
Anne Lamott, *Bird by Bird*
John O'Donohue, *Anam Cara*
John O'Donohue, *Beauty: The Invisible Embrace*
John O'Donohue, *To Bless the Space Between Us*
Eugene Peterson, *The Message*
Jodi Picoult, *Small Great Things*
Richard Rohr, *Falling Upwards*
Richard Rohr, *Immortal Diamond*
Pat Schwiebert and Chuck DeKlyen, *Tear Soup*
Gerry Sitzer, *Grace Disguised*
Dallas Willard, *The Divine Conspiracy: Rediscovering Our Hidden Life in God*
Rowan Williams, *Where God Happens*
William Paul Young, *Lies We Believe About God*
William Paul Young, *The Shack*
Rosamund Stone Zander and Benjamin Zander, *The Art of Possibility*

About the Author

Jocelyn Faire's first book, *Who is Talking Out of My Head?* chronicles her journey of grief as an out of body experience after the tragic accident that took the lives of her two young adult children and a future daughter-in-law. Her writing has been on the InScribe Christian Writers' Fellowship blog, and her own blog (which she confesses has been sporadically maintained):

https://whoistalking.wordpress.com

Jocelyn describes herself as an introverted extrovert, who loves beauty and a good laugh. She studied Creative Writing at the University of Calgary. She delights in grand-mothering, kayaking, beauty, and world travels. She would love to hear from you. Contact her at jbmarietalking@gmail.com

www.ingramcontent.com/pod-product-compliance
Lightning Source LLC
Chambersburg PA
CBHW060400080526
44583CB00012B/411